THE WINNING SIDE

BOOKS BY RALPH DE TOLEDANO

Frontiers of Jazz *(an anthology)*

Seeds of Treason

Spies, Dupes and Diplomats

Day of Reckoning *(a novel)*

Nixon *(a biography)*

Lament for a Generation

The Greatest Plot in History

The Winning Side

THE WINNING SIDE

The Case for Goldwater Republicanism

By

RALPH DE TOLEDANO

G. P. Putnam's Sons

New York

© 1963 by Ralph de Toledano

Library of Congress Catalog
Card Number: 63–20755

MANUFACTURED IN THE UNITED STATES OF AMERICA

For
Zarita Nahon
dear aunt, dearer friend

CONTENTS

INTRODUCTION

The political phenomenon that is Barry Goldwater will intrigue and perplex the wise and the innocent for years to come. Without lifting a finger, he has become the center and the symbol of one of the most unusual political movements in recent history. He is a conservative and therefore, according to the ritualistic response of our times, presumably unpalatable to the "independent" voter and to the intellectual. But the estimable Mr. Gallup, expressing his wonderment, was forced to note that between November 1962 and July 1963, Senator Goldwater's popularity among "independents" had almost tripled.

Mr. Gallup was also constrained to report that among "independents" Goldwater was most liked by those in the 21–49-year group—rather than by the aging Neanderthals of popular myth. The higher the educational bracket, moreover, the greater the Goldwater popularity. Most interesting of all, he was best liked by people in rural communities and in the suburbs—the growing base of today's political strength.

This is not all. In the past, a conservative faded rapidly when any intrepid Liberal exploded under him all the lethal charges of the left-of-center polemics. Yet Goldwater has survived these attacks, perhaps because he seems really not to notice them. Governor Nelson Rockefeller, seeking to force his way back into the Republican Presidential limelight, gathered together the usual descriptives applied to conservatives and hurled them at Senator Goldwater.

If the Goldwater forces took over the Republican Party, the governor warned, it would be "in real danger of subversion by a radical, well-financed and highly disciplined minority" of "extremist groups [utilizing] the tactics of totalitarianism." He called on Goldwater to repudiate the John Birchism before it could "capture" him. All the goblins of the "radical Right" were trotted out to frighten conservatives who were flocking to the Senator's cause.

The Rockefeller warning was picked up by those whose job it is to make issues—even though Goldwater had gone on record in February of 1962 in condemnation of Robert Welch's then-private theory that Dwight David Eisenhower was a secret Communist. "We cannot allow the emblem of irresponsibility to be attached to the conservative banner," said Goldwater in an unsolicited commercial, volunteered after a cold dissection of the Welch thesis in *National Review*.

Senator Goldwater is a phenomenon because he has inspired his audiences to great heights of enthusiasm by the most non-demagogic analyses of the nature of America's problems. There have been times when he has hit out hard, but for the most part he has restored reason as a commodity in the political marketplace. Some of this enthusiasm is generated because Barry Goldwater is instinctively liked, even by those who believe that his opposition to the encroachments of Federal power are the work of a Dr. Faustus (post Infernal bargain).

The junior senator from Arizona did not fade away after the Rockefeller assault, nor did his friends in the press turn their backs on him. And the governor, realizing that he had failed in embarrassing the Goldwater forces, said that all he meant was that he opposed the "radical Right"—a group he delimited as only wanting "to abolish the income tax." Forgotten was the stern rebuke from the gubernatorial mimeograph machine that the Goldwater forces hoped to "erect political power on the outlawed and immoral base of segregation."

That these and other attempts at misrepresenting the nature and thrust of the Goldwater movement fell so flatly is an indication of the impact the senator has had on people of all walks of life, all income brackets, and all ideological persuasions. Decry him they may, but dismiss him they cannot. To a political reporter like myself, he is one of those "naturals" who emerge at critical times. That they emerge because the times call for them is an interesting thought to contemplate.

Barry Goldwater, however, is only tangentially the subject of this book. I believe he will be nominated by the Republican Party and move on to an electoral victory in November 1964. But this is, in a sense, secondary to a thesis of far greater importance—namely, that the Democratic coalition formed by Franklin Delano Roosevelt has begun to come apart and that a new conservative consensus has the potential strength to replace it. Barry Goldwater happens to be eminently equipped for the Presidency—but he is also precisely the candidate who would represent that consensus and re-establish conservatism in the high places of government. This is the significant theme and it is, I believe, amply documented in the pages that follow. That crisis may slow the progress of the conservative movement is always a possibiilty, but this does not touch on the general validity of the thesis.

It is an incontrovertible fact that the stirrings of the two-

party system in the South and the return of the Midwest to
the Republican side have created all the circumstances which
must precede the conservative consensus. Between now and
the Republican convention, there will be an ebb and flow
of Goldwater popularity. There will be times when his
chances may be dimmed by the events and setbacks. There
may even be some bad news in the primaries. But the Goldwater adherents, unlike those who cleave to the other Republican Presidential hopefuls, will not be shaken. Efforts to
"stop Goldwater," as I indicate later on, will fail until a
Liberal Republican candidate is found who can draw to
himself the scattered Rockefeller forces. And such a candidate
is not in the offing.

There is some stirring of sentiment for Richard Nixon, but
this is the product of precisely that Eastern Liberal wing
which has won itself the suspicion of most Republicans.

Let it be firmly noted here that though Goldwater adherents stress the importance of a new consensus in the South,
the Midwest, and the Mountain States, they are not writing
off any region or preparing to lose a single vote by default.
There is Goldwater sentiment in many big cities—and none
of it will be neglected.

In writing this book I have made use of many newspaper
accounts contemporary to the periods touched upon. Since
this is analysis in broad strokes, I will not bore the reader
with a detailed bibliography. I am grateful to M. Stanton
Evans, editor of the Indianapolis *News,* for the statistical
table, pages 112–114, and for valuable suggestions and in-
sights, to William J. Gunn Jr. for his help in research, to
William F. Buckley Jr. for his irrepressible enthusiasm and
encouragement, and to William A. Rusher for urging me to
write this book.

R. de T.

THE WINNING SIDE

I

THE VITAL RIGHT

History moves on wheels of crisis and choice. For the American people at this historical instant, the crisis is grave and the choice is imperative. As citizens of the various states (and therefore of the Federal Union), they must choose between victory and surrender, between national survival and engulfment, between freedom and coercion, between principle and expedience. It is the thesis of this account that the choice has already been made and that it simply awaits the ratification of the voters in an election to come. That choice is for a new era of conservatism based on the interaction of tradition and the contemporary spirit.

The dominant consensus of this country is and has always been of conservative bent. This bent has failed to impose itself on the course of events because forces and individuals have deprived the American people of a choice. But an impatient nation can no longer accept the delay. The lines of battle in what will undoubtedly be a long war are rapidly being drawn up. The reluctant dragons of Liberalism would prefer not to see a confrontation between themselves and the confident St. Georges of conservatism—but they can no longer prevent it.

At stake will be the future of two great parties. The Democratic Party, because of its antecedents and its present commitments to special-interest groups in the Liberal-labor community, can only move Left. The Republican Party, in equal measure, becomes increasingly the national vehicle for American conservatism. Republicanism's more reactionary leaders still cling to tired concepts of "modernism" and cry havoc at the sight of a strong and assertive Right. But their "modernism" is simply a response to the trauma of 1936. They do not see beyond what at the time seemed like the expiring breath of conservatism and the Republican Party.

The Republicans of little and Liberal faith are not aware that in the current political crisis, their party can no longer play at mugwump. If it ignores the choice thrust on it by events, then it is self-condemned to extinction. A political party can survive everything but the loss of its reason for being. At that point, new alignments are made and new parties are formed.

But history is not a blind force. History is made by men who are cast in the role of leadership. The conservative push in America cannot be politically focused without a leader who can bring together the South, the Midwest, the Mountain states, New England, and the Pacific Northwest.

For the first time since the death of Senator Robert A. Taft, such a leader exists. He is, inescapably, Senator Barry Goldwater. Where Taft was a rock, Goldwater is the flint and steel which can strike fire in the electorate. For the first time in decades, it can be said with certainty that conservatism is the winning side—but only if its will to win is not compromised by Republican Liberalism. By recognizing that a crisis exists and that a choice must be made, millions of Americans have taken the first step. The next step is to convert their optimism into earnest organizational activity. Awareness of the issues has created a new urgency.

The traditional safeguards which prevented tyrannies of the majority or the minority have been steadily eroded by more than thirty years of government centralization and juridical whimsy. Those basic documents of American freedom, the Constitution and the Declaration of Independence, have been torn up by a nationalized Supreme Court which substitutes sociology and Executive "need" for the rule of law and precedent. The Bill of Rights, written by the Founding Fathers to protect the states and their individual citizens from oppressive governments, has been replaced by the amorphous Rights of Man—a starry-eyed document which gave justification to the Terror and the guillotine of the French Revolution even as it proclaimed its love of justice.

Within the Federal Establishment, the Congress has been systematically downgraded by an Executive Branch which, as it ingests more and more power, becomes more and more corrupting of itself. The two-party system has been weakened and is today threatened. In the past, both parties tolerated an ideological consensus. That there had been no polarization which placed every Liberal in one camp, every conservative in the other, was justly credited as a stabilizer of the American political system. But in recent years, as the hapless voter found out, it ceased to be a consensus. By careful propaganda, doctrinaire Liberals almost succeeded in imposing a rigid New Conformity on both parties. Only the essential strength of the American political system—and the stubborn resistance of the American dedication—prevented the imposition of an ideological straitjacket. Control of the mass media and the educational process has been utilized to disenfranchise the Center and Right.

The nation's foreign policy has been conducted without any real debate by the electorate or their duly elected representatives in the Congress. For the Liberal ideologues, the consensus has been *their* consensus—and woe unto the man who challenges their sublime faith in the efficacy of "negotiation" with Communism, in the superiority of socializing governments, in the losing of friends and the influencing of practically nobody, and in their deep-rooted suspicion of things and people anti-Communist. Herblock, the Washington *Post*'s brilliant but unconscionable political cartoonist, feels fully justified in spraying with acid and black ink all who even look longingly to an *appertura alla destra*—an opening to the Right.

But the trend which brought on the Liberal monopoly has been reversed. A new generation, which knew not Franklin Delano Roosevelt, is on the move. On college campuses, in the meeting halls and the homes of those who have begun their life's work with a coercive state looming, and those who early or late saw that under the pancake makeup of the New/Fair Deals and the New Frontier the complexion of today's Liberalism was pocked, the realization grows that the issue is survival—survival for the nation and for those who make up its citizenry, survival at home and in the world of nations. It is from these new conservatives that the cadres have trained their troops, making them effectives in the battle to reinvigorate American freedom. It is these troops that can bring about an era of prosperity and good feeling such as this Union has never known. The impact on the public consciousness of Senator Goldwater is a symptom of the American renascence.

Equally significant for those who believe in the American purpose is the transformation that has occurred within the

Congress. The House of Representatives, once the less stable and more Liberal body—and certainly the one most susceptible to pressure from the Executive and other special-interest groups—has emerged as the custodian of tradition. It has fought as well as it could for fiscal responsibility. And it has rebelled against the cavalier treatment by the Supreme Court of the Constitution and of the system of checks and balances, holding the line as best it can against a Senate whose greater prestige has been put at the disposal of the White House and its semiofficial lobbyists. That the House of Representatives should take over the responsibilities of the Senate to act as a brake on ill-considered and ill-conceived action is of great importance, for its members have always been handily responsive to the popular will. In part, the House's posture has been conditioned by young and articulate legislators whose views are of increasing importance in shaping conservative Republican policy.* That most of them come from the Midwest indicates the full return of that region to the Republican fold.

The rise throughout the country of what has been disparagingly called the New Conservatism, the inroads it has begun to make within the once hermetical Liberal academic community, and the phenomenal response to those uncompromising spokesmen for sound American principles who are not gagged and bound over to political oblivion are clear indications that the day of reckoning is at hand for the careless receivers of the country's future. The accelerating pace of the South as it advances on two-party government—and the election of Republican conservatives in districts once safely

* Melvin Laird and John Byrnes of Wisconsin, Gerald Ford of Michigan, Thomas Curtis of Missouri, John Rhodes of Arizona, and Donald Bruce of Indiana, to name but several.

Democratic—are part of the prognosis. But the test and the demonstration will come in the elections of 1964, 1966, and 1968, as the conservative armies wheel around the walls of Jericho. Not all at once but decisively, it will be made manifest that the conservative bent of the American majority can be employed to frustrate the rampaging minorities now determining public policy.

As the winning side drives to victory, the first battleground will be the Republican Party. The reasons for this are at once complex and simple, as the ensuing chapters of this account will demonstrate. Briefly stated, they break down into two major points:

1. The Democratic Party is now the instrument of a Liberal-Left coalition. Since the War Between the States, it has sustained itself on the legitimate Southern resentment to the excesses of the Reconstruction. But its political heart has belonged to big-city minority groups and to ambitious ideologues who could see no future for themselves in the extremist and Marxist-Leninist parties.

2. Whatever the election results of the past decades may seem to indicate—or the Gallup Poll proclaim—the Republican Party has represented a real or potential majority of the electorate. The battle for America must therefore first be fought to recapture the Republican Party from those whose heart's desire seems to be to make it a pallid twin of the Democratic Party. Once this battle has been won, the confrontation of Left and Right can take place. In 1940, 1944, 1948, 1952, 1956, and 1960, clear-cut distinctions were obscured. The voter seeking a Liberal candidate settled for the real article and not for the Republocratic imitation. The conservative voter knew that he was not being given a signifi-

cant choice. If he worked at all for the Republican Party, it was out of habit or for Auld Lang Syne.

I believe that by far the harder task for Repulican conservatives will be the recapture of the party machinery. Once this is accomplished then their candidates will have a chance to go to the voters and to prove the validity of the conservative thesis.

The question nevertheless remains: How did a minority of ideologues so nearly succeed in remaking the Republican Party in their own image? Since the days of Samuel Adams, there has always been a streak of Jacobinism in America—and the levelers have not been an entirely alien group. But there have been very few periods in which this streak has been little more than a sign of the nation's political multiplicity. Until 1933, the major exception was the Jacksonian era. In the not-too-distant past Know-Nothingism never did more than stir the waters of American polity.

In a book, *The Vital Center,* written before divinity and a White House business address had settled on him, Arthur M. Schlesinger, Jr., confessed that "in a fundamental sense" the so-called middle position of Liberalism "itself represent[s] one extreme." To the right of the extremism of the Vital Center, Schlesinger deposited most of what remained of a nation which, it seemed to him, was controlled by the "forces of corruption." This formulation is of considerable pertinence in assessing the retreat of the conservatives. Only when it is thoroughly demolished can there be any really Vital Right.

For if the Vital Center is itself an extreme, then it follows that the conservative Right is centrist—and beyond that lies the crackpot fringe so dear to the heart of Democratic propagandists. The ideological spectrum, in its acceptable colorations, is therefore drastically foreshortened. On the one hand, there are Schlesinger's extremist Liberals and opposing them are the milk-and-water conservatives—the "modern Republicans" who differ as a rule only in party label from their Democratic antagonists. The ambitious candidate, convinced that conservatism is the kiss of death and the mark of Cain, stubbornly closes his right eye and attempts to see through his nose. (This may account for the high casualty rate among Republicans.)

As a result of this kind of thinking, assiduously promoted by the Democratic politburo and its evangels in the press, the American conservative movement has found itself in the past decades deprived of its franchise. This was ironically true even during the years of the Eisenhower Administration, when the Vital Right was steadily growing in numbers and establishing a beachhead in the academic community. The same attitude persists today among many in the Republican Party's national leadership and among some of its Congressional spokesmen. The crypto-liberals of the GOP share a slight queasiness over conservatism because they have been convinced that it is doomed to endless defeat. And the staff of the Republican National Committee seems always about to sign a nonaggression pact with its Democratic counterpart. They all have tacitly accepted the Schlesingerist doctrine.

Life, however, has a stronger voice than those of the theorizers. The idea that the Vital Right is a creation of the wishful thinkers and the crackpot fringe has been rudely challenged by the nation's voting trends in the past elections. With growing frequency, "hard" conservatives have triumphed whereas the glamour boys of "modern Republican" stripe have with equal frequency been defeated or come dangerously close to it by lackluster candidates of the Liberal-

Left. Because political concepts filter slowly to the public consciousness, the thought has only now begun to reach a few intrepid thinkers that for Republicans the conservative side is the winning side—not as we have been told for several decades, that it must inevitably lose. This is a revolutionary apperception in this decade of the twentieth century, and its effect has so far been electric.

The conflict between the Vital Right and the Murky Middle will come to a climax in 1964. But the forces facing each other will not merely represent ideological positions. A regional conflict will also be evident. On the one hand can can be found the Eastern Liberal wing of the Republican Party, in the thrall of Europe-oriented financial interests. Opposed to it are the Midwest, areas of the Pacific Northwest, northern New England, and the South—all basically middle class economically, more than less homogenous, and not yet ready to abdicate their political rights to a congeries of special pleaders or to open their veins to the New Conformity's tired-blood bank.

If, in 1964, the Republican Party should fail to declare its independence of the Eastern political moguls who now corrupt its thinking—if it should brush aside the mandate of those who formed the party—it will doom itself to the role of feeble opposition and eventual extinction. Like the Whigs of another period, the Republicans will see their strength whittled away. The Congressional contingent may, for a time, cling to the old label. But politics, like nature, abhors a vacuum. The Republican irregulars in Congress will, at best, fight a rear-guard action. In the country as a whole, Republicanism will succumb to a new party or be swallowed up entire by Mr. Schlesinger's vital extreme.

The second alternative will mean the end of two-party

government in the United States and the consolidation of the Coercive State which the eminent liberal historian, Vernon Parrington, saw emerging from the doctrinaire Leftism of the New Deal's forerunners. No party can exist in permanent opposition, carping at those in the seats of power and repeating slogans of empty defiance. Nor can any party command the respect of the electorate if it simply veers one degree to the right of the entrenched Left. This is particularly true of Republicanism whose strength has traditionally derived from the Midwest, from New England, from pockets of resistance in the Border States—and nationally from the homogeneity of deeply rooted middle-class Americans. In this day and time, the Republican Party cannot cringe before the shrews of Eastern Liberalism and still develop strong and necessary ties with the new and enlightened conservative South—a South rapidly recovering from the morphine addiction of the Franklin D. Roosevelt cult and the Federal handout.

In the past, reasonable men might have argued over the merits of conservative versus Park Avenue (or Princeton) Republicanism as a means of winning elections—even though the record was not a happy one for the Eastern Liberal kingmakers. They lost with Wendell Willkie, despite the built-in advantage of the two-term issue, because to grass-roots Republicans he was just what Harold Ickes called him, "the barefoot boy from Wall Street." They failed with Thomas E. Dewey because the voters felt that his political utterances were, as Willkie openly admitted of his own, "campaign oratory." This writer was present at a private dinner in February of 1951 at one of New York's exclusive clubs when the powers of Eastern Republicanism—Winthrop Aldrich and others—in effect nominated Dwight D. Eisenhower, simply because he was the only man capable of stopping the late Senator Robert A. Taft. Richard Nixon, who tried to link the conservatives and the Liberals in the Republican Party, lost by a hair because the potential strength which would have been thrown into the balance had he forthrightly followed his own bent was inhibited.

What the Eastern kingmakers never knew and therefore could not remember is that the Republican Party was created more by the issue of "sixty acres and a mule" and the Homestead Act than by the searing rhetoric of the Abolitionists or the radical doctrines of Eastern intellectuals who attached themselves to the infant political organism. It was the radical wing of the Republican Party which poisoned American history for a century by imposing the Reconstruction on the defeated South. And it has been the present cabal of Eastern "modern Republicans" who have permitted the party to come apart at the seams organizationally.

Conversely, the Republican Party has prospered when its governance was in the hands of political professionals who came from less ideologically polluted areas than Manhattan. Mark Hanna in another day and Ray Bliss in ours, both of Ohio, can be held up as practitioners of successful Republicanism. Today the frontier has moved farther West, but there is no Republican who understands the mechanics of political operation better than Senator Barry Goldwater of Arizona, perhaps because he is unequivocally a party man yet stands as a symbol—the Mr. Conservative of these troubled days.

In contrast, the Eastern-endorsed group of Presidential hopefuls is neither fish, nor fowl, nor good red herring. However admirable they may be as men and as local leaders, they lack ideological definition. Is Governor George Romney of Michigan sound on the issues which today divide America?

Is Governor William Scranton, charming and sincere, within the Vital Center or the Vital Right? Is Governor Nelson Rockefeller of New York a prisoner of the Left or a spokesman for the Right? That the questions are asked condemns these would-be tenants of 1600 Pennsylvania Avenue. Despite massive attempts to obscure Goldwater's position, it is known. The voter can take it or leave it. There is nothing amorphous about it. No one can ask of him—as they asked of Richard Nixon, though perhaps unfairly—where he stands. And this inspires confidence in his ability to take the offensive, to end the crisis in American politics, and to make known the choice of the electorate.

Given the wholehearted support of his party and a strategy which makes use of conservative strengths and Liberal weaknesses—not vice versa—Barry Goldwater can win. But simply in asserting his candidacy and making the battle for the Presidency he will be doing the country a service. The Eastern kingmakers are dead but they won't lie down. Whatever historical energy allowed them to seize the leadership of the Republican Party has by now petered out. Economic power has permitted them to put pressures on the Republican convention and to hijack control of the quadrennial event. But nowhere in the fifty states, with the possible exception of New York, do they hold the reins of the party organization. They can at best bludgeon, and this is hardly the way to lasting political success in a free society. Time after time, it has been demonstrated that the Republican Party—at the grassroots, precinct, county, and to a very large degree the state levels—has accepted the domineering of the Eastern Liberal wing because it was told that "a conservative can't win" and that only a Liberal could.

The arithmetic was against the "modern" Republicans—

but they succeeded in their big dream of dominating Presidential nominating conventions.

Barry Goldwater, whose political successes and wide following run counter to all the "rules," has demolished the false arguments of anti-conservatism. There are some who say he cannot achieve the Presidency. But each day brings new testimony from friend and foe that in any contest, he would be the strongest candidate the Republican Party could field. The Eastern Liberal wing finds itself on the defensive. Knowing that you can't stop somebody with nobody, it shops desperately for a counter-Goldwater, hopefully scanning lists of military heroes who might be able to duplicate General Eisenhower's performance. It is all very dispiriting for the kingmakers.

For the true heirs of the Republican Party, and for the Barry Goldwater who marches with them, it is a heady experience to know that they are on the winning side. With each step down the road to the 1964 convention, history is being made. Millions of Americans, once apathetic, stir with new excitement. They feel that for the first time in decades, their votes will count and their wishes will be respected. Every special election shows a record outpouring of voters— a sign that politics has again assumed a meaning and a place in American life.

But conservative Republicans—and conservative Democrats who this year or next will find a new political home—are aware that enthusiasm is not enough. The Vital Right must be armed with the facts. It must know where to press and how to organize. The blueprint for 1964 and beyond cannot be drawn or understood without carefully reading the handwriting on 1962's wall.

II

SURPRISE IN 1962

In 1962, as in other election years, the pundits sharpened their adjectives and polished their deep thoughts long before the voters wandered in and out of polling places. As usual, the pundits were certain that all their *a priori* judgments would be vindicated by the electorate. All the good little Liberals would win, the conservatives would sniffle as they came out of the political woodshed, the Kennedy Administration would come up all over roses. Only those Republicans who made it clear that their ideology belonged to Big Daddy in Washington would go to their temporal reward. As usual, too, that Liberal article of faith—"nobody shoots Santa Claus"—would remain the basic tenet of our times.

And so it was that the 1962 election was interpreted by the lazy and the eager. The pundits took a look at the statistics, shuffled them about, and announced that President Kennedy was the big winner. In an off year, he had managed to cut down his losses in the House of Representatives to an unprecedented two seats. In the Senate he had more violently shattered tradition by actually picking up strength. California returned Senator Thomas Kuchel to Washington by a thumping plurality and New York did ditto for Senator Jacob Javits. Both men represented that most complete iden-

tification with Liberal policies—and seemingly their only con-
nection with the Republican Party to which they nominally
belonged was in the label. Beyond that, they would have
been undistinguishable from those about them at a meeting
of Americans for Democratic Action. In California, too,
Richard Nixon came a cropper as he attempted simultaneously to ride the horses of Liberalism and conservatism.
Here and there, conservatism scored an upset and unlikely
Republicans won—but there were explanations in plenty
from the pundits for this phenomenon, as there always are.

The fact, of course, was that the 1962 election in its own
way marked a milestone in American political history as important as the 1930 election which began the fragmentation
of the Republican Party and set the stage for the advent of
the New Deal. President Kennedy's victory was more apparent than real, although it took the pundits and analysts some
time to find this out. As William A. Rusher would write in
National Review:

America's most accomplished tea-leaf readers have now con-
cluded their study of the November election results, and they are
turning up with an interpretation so unexpected and so unsettling
that many of them profoundly wish they had never investigated
the matter at all.

This was a remarkable understatement. For the results
demonstrated that President Kennedy and his party were in
for real trouble. Far more devastating, they torpedoed right
out of the water the stubbornly accepted belief that "only"
a Liberal Republican could win in 1964 or 1968. In fact, the
conclusion shared by the most punctilious analysts was to
precisely the opposite point. The star of Governor Nelson
Rockefeller, till then on the ascendant, showed signs of run-

ning out of liquid oxygen—something that political stars must always have in abundance. And for the first time, the opportunists in both parties—usually the last to get the news —began to look at Senator Barry Goldwater calculatingly. The tolerant smiles on Liberal faces which had greeted talk of the conservative resurgence in America turned suddenly to frowns. And more than one Liberal Republican wondered if his Keynes was showing.

Counting noses on Capitol Hill and his blessings at 1600 Pennsylvania Avenue, the President could make out a good case for Democratic assertions that his party had done well at the polls. But a more penetrating look at the election statistics indicated that the Democratic Party might have to admit its minority position if the trend continued. It took only a moderate amount of Republican exuberance to argue that the GOP was in certain ways a disenfranchised majority— deprived of its patrimony by political passions dating back to the Reconstruction Era and now turned markedly tepid.

The statistics which startled the politicians were hard to answer. Because of the makeup of Republican and Democratic areas, it takes 100,000 votes to put a member of Mr. Kennedy's party in the House of Representatives. It takes 137,000 votes to put a Republican in the House. This is an immediate advantage for the Democrats—but there are others of greater import. Since the War Between the States, the Democratic Party, however unrepresentative of the non-urban areas it may be, has always started out with the Southern vote in its pocket. Until recently only foolhardy or vainglorious Republicans ran for office south of the Mason and Dixon Line. The 1962 election showed that the winds of change—if we agree that *plus ça change, plus c'est la même chose*—had changed the political configuration of the South.

In the North, the Republican Party hurt from the inroads of the Kennedy Dollar in New England, and suffered a loss of 4.3 percentage points. But in the 39 non-Southern States, the Grand Old Party was able to chalk up a very respectable 49.5 percent of the vote, despite the New England setback. This was a more-than-tidy increase of 15.7 percent at a time when the Democratic vote declined slightly (0.15 percent). On the Pacific Coast, the Republican vote was 870,000 over what it had been in 1958—the previous by-election—whereas the Democrats dropped 17,000. In the West North Central states, the GOP picked up 211,000 votes and the Democrats lost 206,000. In the Mountain states the Republicans picked up an additional 247,000 over 1958, while Democrats were forced to content themselves with an increase of 19,000.

But what of the South? In politics, Newton's Third Law ("every action has an equal and opposite reaction") is partially applicable. By that I mean that when a party or a candidate puts on a strong and stirring campaign, the opposition profits simply because voters who might have stayed at home go to the polls. Republican inroads in the South brought out the voters, and the Democrats picked up an extra 1.1 million votes, or 41 percent. The Republican growth, however, was 244 percent—from 606,000 votes in 1958 to 2,084,000 in 1962. As the Republican National Committee said:

Major Republican gains were made in every Southern state with the exception of Mississippi where there were no Republican candidates. These gains ranged from a 9.2 percentage point increase in the Republican vote in Florida to 32.0 points in Texas. In three Southern states—North Carolina, Texas, and Virginia—Republicans won 40 percent or more of the total vote.

Republican and Democratic strategists, hardly susceptible to the wishful fulminations of the pundits, viewed the startling rise of Republican strength in the South as more than a passing fancy of the voters. It was matched by the organizational success of candidates to a variety of offices. The idea that Southerners voted Republican in fear and trembling, looking anxiously over their shoulders for the pitchfork of a Yankee devil, suddenly lost even the most poetic validity. Dreary arguments that General Eisenhower had made substantial inroads into the Southern Democratic monolith only because he was a war hero, that the election from Texas of John Tower to the Senate was a freak, and that the steady increase in an admittedly modest list of GOP officeholders was hardly a trend suddenly seemed very hollow. The dramatic rise in Republican strength in the old states of the Confederacy was even more remarkable when measured against the fact that the GOP failed to field candidates in 50 out of 106 districts.

The 1962 results in the South premised much for the Republican future. The GOP votes came from the sector of the electorate most likely to assume a dominant role in years to come—the urban middle class. Liberal pundits of both parties rushed to warn the Republicans that they must not attempt to "outbid" the segregationist forces in seeking the Southern vote. The plain fact, however, is that Democratic strength in the South in 1962 has increasingly been based on an unlikely combination of the Negro and the rural segregationist vote. In Alabama, for example, where a GOP unknown, James Martin, came within 6,800 votes of defeating veteran Senator Lister Hill, the Republican candidate carried every major city, with an average in counties of 100,000 or more of 53.6. In the remaining counties, where segregationist feeling runs high, Martin polled 46.2 percent of the vote.

The same pattern was discernible in South Carolina where Democratic Senator Olin Johnston carried 14 of the 20 counties which went to the States' Rights party in 1956. The Republican senatorial candidate received 48.4 of the vote in the urban counties, only 38.1 percent in the countryside. The relationship of racial tension to Democratic success was most markedly pinpointed in Texas. In the gubernatorial race, Democrat John Connally carried 59 of 65 counties on record as opposing integration 5-to-1. Republican Jack Cox carried six. In counties which were 10-to-1 for segregation, Cox's vote fell far below his average for the state. All surveys of the 1962 election showed that Southerners turned to the Republican Party because they opposed the economic policies of the Kennedy Administration and the national Democratic Party. Race was at most a tangential issue except with the white, rural, low-income voter who considered the Negro a rival for his job.

In both North and South, the Republicans could take confidence from the vote in suburban areas. The voter turnout was more than half a million above 1958, for a growth of 14 percent.

A study of thirteen metropolitan areas showed a rise in the Republican vote in all but two of these major suburbs. And those shadows on an otherwise bright conservative picture were, paradoxically, portents of the conservative resurgence. In both cases, the Republicans had compromised their position by running candidates who belonged to their party's Liberal wing. In the New York suburbs, the electorate contemplated Governor Nelson Rockefeller and Senator Jacob Javits—and there was a 2.5 percent drop in the vote. In the

Boston suburban area, the candidacy of George Lodge, who hoped to win the seat once held by his father in the United States Senate, was not one to inspire electoral passions. Lodge lost ignominiously to Edward Kennedy, the President's younger brother—as well he should have. With no differences of principle, any voter would cast his ballot for the man who seemed most likely to bring patronage to Massachusetts.

Interestingly enough, in eight of the suburban areas studied, the Republicans showed greater gains than they did statewide. This was dramatically manifest in Michigan, where George Romney broke the stranglehold of the Democratic Party and of UAW President Walter Reuther on the governorship. In 1958 the Republican candidate had trailed by 225,000 votes in Detroit, by 76,000 in the Detroit suburbs. The 154,000 advantage in the rest of the state could not make up for this 301,000-vote deficit. But in 1962 the deficit in suburban Detroit turned into a plurality of 34,000, for a percentage increase of 8.8, whereas statewide the Republican increase was 2.9 percent.

In the cities themselves, the Republican vote showed the beginning of an upward trend. Of eleven cities which had given Richard Nixon less than 40 percent of the vote in the 1960 Presidential election, eight showed substantial gains in gubernatorial races. The most noteworthy was in Cleveland, Ohio, which gave James A. Rhodes 17 percentage points more than it had given Nixon. In this case, the improvement was due to two factors: the work of State Chairman Ray Bliss who began working for 1962 before all the 1960 ballots had been counted, thereby continuing to rebuild a once-shattered Ohio GOP, and the clear-cut conservatism of the candidate. In Congressional races, the Republicans also made gains in the cities, though the Democrats for the most part still remained in fairly safe control. What was of considerable importance in gauging future political activity was the stagnancy of the big-city vote. Ten cities, including some of the nation's largest, increased their turnout by only 59,000 votes. During this period, statewide totals rose. Increasingly, therefore, the balance of power had begun to move to suburbs in which the GOP was strong. And since the totals for these cities showed a Republican gain of 135,000, against a Democratic decline of 76,000, the GOP's urban prospects could not be said to be as gloomy as some pundits read them.

In the farm areas, the Republican Party snapped back from its slump. In only two states, North Dakota and Idaho, did the farm vote decline in pivotal counties. In twelve states, it showed moderate to great gains. A survey of 88 farm counties in the fourteen states showed that Republican congressional candidates took 57.5 percent of the 1962 vote, or 7.6 percentage points more than the numbing 49.9 percent of 1958 when the party's predominance in agricultural communities seemed a thing of the past. This reversal of a trend contributed to GOP successes as the party hit the comeback trail to the state houses. The low point had been 1958, when the Republicans were reduced to fourteen governors and only seven states in which they controlled both houses of the legislature. In 1962, sixteen Republican governors were elected, and it included a return to the fold of such powerhouse states as Ohio, Pennsylvania, and Michigan. In eighteen states, the GOP restored its grip on both houses of the legislature.

The gubernatorial races in the powerhouse states were particularly gratifying to Republicans in the matter of comparative voting. Ohio, the home of Senator Robert A. Taft and the birthplace of Presidents, had mustered barely 43.1

percent of the vote in 1958 for a Republican gubernatorial candidate. James Rhodes, with the happy help of State Chairman Bliss, rolled up 58.9 percent. Pennsylvania had jumped from 48.9 to 55.4 percent. In Oklahoma, the results were almost incredible. In 1958 the Republican candidate had limped in with a sad 20 percent of the vote. A determined group of Republican conservatives had vowed to change that —and so they did. By working tirelessly, building up strength on the precinct level, and by infusing his colleagues with an undeviating enthusiasm, Henry Bellmon won the governorship with 55.3 percent—the first Republican to hold that office in the state's history. His victory nailed home the fact that the one-party South was a thing of the past.

Perhaps the most closely watched state was New York where Nelson Rockefeller, chief pretender to the Republican Presidential nomination, was seeking a second gubernatorial term. Governor Rockefeller was expected to win—and big! He had been campaigning long before the Democrats had chosen their candidate. New York Democrats were still not recovered from a Kennedy Administration blitz which drove out their old leaders and installed a so-called reform group. The Rockefeller opposition was the inexperienced and unknown Edward Morgenthau, selected by the White House as a kind of sacrificial lamb for the expected slaughter, whose candidacy was so uninspired that he made the newspapers only because of an editorial tradition that requires something like equal treatment.

Until Election Day, Governor Rockefeller's managers were predicting a sweep of such proportions—an 800,000 plurality —that no one would be able to contest his claims to the Presidential nomination. The sweep materialized—but not for Mr. Rockefeller. Though the Republicans added to their màjority in the legislature and increased their vote in 27 of the state's 41 congressional districts, Governor Rockefeller's showing was by any standard feeble. His built-in advantage as the incumbent availed him nothing. In fact, he polled 43,865 votes *less* than when he ran against Governor Averell Harriman. A determined new Conservative Party cut into his vote by 141,877. When the votes of his opponents were added up, Governor Rockefeller's plurality was whittled down to a sad 357,832 votes—hardly a sign of popular enthusiasm.

To make matters worse, Senator Jacob Javits' margin over his opponents was 851,717. Even Governor Rockefeller's Attorney General Louis Lefkowitz, certainly no great vote getter, could boast of a 602,935 margin. Since the gubernatorial race drew substantially more votes than other state-wide contests, Governor Rockefeller's showing was that much sadder. He had spent over $2 million and called on the help of advisers, speech writers, and drumbeaters from the Rockefeller businesses and foundation—their wages not included in regular campaign costs. The Democrats admitted to spending but $420,000, a fifth of the Rockefeller total.

The 1962 elections cast doubt on Governor Rockefeller's putative appeal to the voters. But they ended former Vice-President Richard Nixon's chance of a second attempt at the Presidency. Nixon was roundly defeated in California by Governor Edmund (Pat) Brown—a political would-be with as much charm as an unsuccessful used-car dealer. The Nixon defeat proved that California, once a Democratic state with perennial Republican officeholders, had fallen victim to the Liberal-labor coalition. It also proved that once more the Republicans had been caught short. Governor Brown's success could be directly attributed to an innovation in California politics. For the first time, the volunteers who

traditionally furnished both parties with most of their electoral manpower were replaced on the Democratic side by
paid workers who corralled lackadaisical voters and trans-
ported them to polling places.

Far more significant than the elimination of a potential
Republican Presidential candidate, the California results
were bad news for the Eastern Liberal wing of the party.
Even as the Rockefeller showing had written off New York
as one of the states the GOP could count on in 1964, so
Nixon's defeat removed California from the projected tally—
if a Liberal Republican ran. For Republican Liberals, this
was bad news indeed. Without California and New York,
they could no longer claim that the GOP must subvert its
policies to appeal to these states. For Republican conservatives—the overwhelming majority of the party—it meant that
the chances for a new consensus, based on a coalition of
Southern, Midwestern, and Mountain states, was for the first
time in decades possible.

When all the votes had been counted, George Gallup sent
his pollsters out to corroborate what the election tallies had
shown. Among what groups, they sought to learn, had the
Republicans made inroads into Democratic strength? The
Gallup answers were a surprise both to the professionals and
the pundits. Samplings of all population groups seemed to
show that, except among the Negroes and the Catholics, the
Republicans had made measurable advances. The Catholic
vote, according to the Gallup poll figures, had remained un-
changed. Among Negroes there had been a 5 percentage point
drop. The Republican Protestant vote had risen 8 points to
59 percent. The Jewish vote, at 28 percent, had risen 12
points. For the first time in many years, the white collar
workers had crossed over to the Republican side 51-to-49.

College graduates chalked up a solid 65 percent, up 11 points, for the GOP. Even among those whose education did not go beyond grade school, the tally was 41 percent—up 8 points. Independent voters, the darlings of the pundits, gave the GOP a one percentage point majority.

To the professionals, the political strategists, and the men who look beyond the headline for the fact, this statistical analysis of the 1962 election was no index to future easy victories. (In politics, there are no easy victories.) But it did answer those who spoke of Republican "defeat" and Democratic "victory." *Time* magazine, with something like prescience, had said in its post-election issue:

Democratic enthusiasts claimed victory—they called it "commanding," "massive," "smashing," and "a landslide." Some landslide. In arithmetical terms, the off-year elections of 1962 were almost a standoff. And in their portent to U. S. politics for the next two years, they meant difficult legislative going for the Democratic Kennedy Administration and the possibility of real trouble in 1964.

In cold, hard terms, it was hardly a standoff. It came after a Kennedy election "victory" which had cost the Democrats 21 House seats in 1960—an unprecedented situation. The President himself could take what comfort he could from his popularity rating in Dr. George Gallup's soothing samplings. But he was a minority President, carried into office by the stolen votes of the Daley machine in Chicago, the Lyndon Johnson instant landsliders in Texas, and the empty but counted acres of an incompleted urban renewal project in St. Louis. Only the tolerance of the South had sustained him in 1960. Without the South, 1964 was a bleak vista for the Democratic Party. And what the South showed in 1962 was a determination to restore to itself prerogatives lost when it put on blinkers and unquestioningly hauled the national Democratic Party's wagon.

In its economic principles, in its devotion to Constitutional government, and in its abhorrence for any tyranny (whether of majorities or minorities), the South was kin to the Midwest, to the Mountain states, to the American countryside. In this, it was as Republican as John C. Calhoun, Robert A. Taft, and Barry Goldwater.

This association of hopes, desires, and principles had no relationship to the racial and political hatred engendered by Northern and Southern demagogues. It was American to the root. And it took 1962 to make this fact understood and accepted by those whose honest partisanship had resulted in willful blindness. In 1962, what the pre-New Deal past had been—and what the post-New Frontier would be—suddenly reached the consciousness of millions of Americans. It was all there in the conservative Republican consensus which once governed the United States of America.

III

REPUBLICANS VS. DEMOCRATS—
THE LONG VIEW

The 1962 election came as a bad shock to the Democrats. They had seen the gradual mend of Republican fortunes after the cataclysm of 1936 and the Landon defeat. The culmination of this trend had seemed to be the election of Dwight David Eisenhower in 1952 and his reelection in 1956. And even the Eisenhower victories had been compromised by the loss of Congress to the Democrats in 1954—a loss from which there seemed no hope of recovery. The decline and fall of Richard Nixon was taken by Democratic strategists as the beginning of another Republican toboggan slide. It did not penetrate that Nixon's failure to win the Presidency had been marked by John F. Kennedy's somewhat pitiable victory and a loss of twenty-one seats in the House of Representatives. Certainly, it was recognized that President Kennedy could not look out at the Inaugural crowds and claim a mandate. He was a man who had squeaked through to the world's highest office with a minority vote and the suspicion that vote frauds in Texas, Illinois, and Missouri were the margin of his success.

The 1962 election was of true importance only to those

who studied the returns with an eye to the past and an understanding of the present. Leaving the South aside, the Republican consensus seemed once more to be forming—and in very much the manner that it had existed since the turn of the century. The old areas of Republican strength, submerged by the Roosevelt tidal wave, were once more beginning to thrust themselves above tidewater levels. The Eisenhower victories were in a sense abnormal to the course of the trend and they were in no real sense political. General Eisenhower was a war hero and a man of such overwhelming personal appeal that his success at the polls had little relation to party programs and party voting. In any long-run sense, he contributed to Republican progress only by helping to remove the Southern inhibition to vote outside the Democratic fold. In 1928, many Southerners had bolted, joining Herbert Hoover's procession to the White House. But there had been reprisals. After 1952, it became apparent that jumping over the fence did not mean political suicide. The transition was made easy because only die-hard ideologues considered President Eisenhower a Republican. Only at the end of his Administration did he consider himself anything but "President of all the people."

But Eisenhower aside, the Republican Party was steadily returning (with some setbacks) to the majority status it enjoyed for many years. Between 1888 and 1960, the Republicans had polled over 50 percent of the popular vote in nine Presidential elections. The Democrats during that period had won a majority only four times—for the four Roosevelt terms. All the vaunted strength of the minorities in the big cities and the special-interest voters who flocked to the Democratic Party were not enough to give it half the popular vote. Deducting the Solid South, Democratic claims to a national mandate simply evaporated. The only Democratic victory between 1896, William McKinley's year, and the Great Depression was Woodrow Wilson's. Yet he won in 1912 with less than 42 percent of the vote, and in 1916 with 49.3 percent. In 1948 and 1960, the Democrats were able to win only by spotting their votes strategically and barricading themselves in the Electoral College. As strategies go, it was an excellent one. (It can be followed by other parties which, in this instance, will feel no compunction about saying, "Me, too.")

When the Republican Party elected McKinley in 1896, it polled 51 percent of the vote—its first majority in close to a quarter of a century—against William Jennings Bryan's 47 percent. It has become something of a joke to mention McKinley, as if he represented reaction rampant or the last gasp of fogyism. But the joke is as unfair as it is stale. McKinley and his alter ego, Marcus Alonzo Hanna, would have been better treated by history had they not been responsible for the political destruction of the Great Commoner. Democracy's supreme impostor, as H. L. Mencken called him, Bryan certainly was that—and obviously unable to understand the issues of the day. Like so many professional lovers of mankind, however, he generated political hatreds as he went along, and McKinley was the target.

Henry Adams saw McKinley as the apostle of capitalism, which was inaccurate. Bridging the era between the last frontier and the beginning of America's manifest leap into world affairs, McKinley represented the kind of careful and enlightened conservatism which marked this country's basic thinking. He believed in the individual and he opposed all concepts of the class struggle. Like Mark Hanna, he could not abide terminology which divided people into "lower" and "upper" classes. It has been forgotten that what brought the two men together and made of them an invincible political team was a litigation in which young McKinley defended twenty-four strikers who had destroyed property at one of Hanna's mines in their efforts to get at strikebreakers. McKinley won acquittal for twenty-three of the strikers. He also won the friendship of Hanna, who saw in the young lawyer the makings of a President.*

The importance of McKinley and Hanna to this account stems from their contribution to Republican politics. In the sad days after the 1948 election, this was recalled by Wilfred Binkley in *Fortune* magazine, who urged conservatives to "study the incomparable party leadership of Marcus A. Hanna, the businessman's finest contribution to the art of politics." In Hanna's rule book, the candidate had to be a man of stature and one who inspired confidence, and McKinley had both these qualifications. In the day before the ghost writer and the prepared text, he had to be a speaker whose sincerity could hold audiences—and Senator Robert La Follette testified to McKinley's outstanding abilities as an orator. He had to be known—and two years before the nominating convention McKinley toured the Republican states on a special train equipped, for the first time in political history, with a press car. (It was during this campaign swing that he demonstrated what contemporary accounts would proclaim: the ability to win over the so-called average man and to control the politicians.)

* Hanna, the secretary of the miner's union testified in 1876, "was the first mining operator in the bituminous fields to recognize the cardinal principle of arbitration in the settlement of wage disputes and the first to recognize" the miner's union. He also made a scene at the Cleveland Union Club over George Pullman's refusal to negotiate the bitter railroad strike brought on by a wage cut. "A man who won't meet his men halfway is a damned fool," Hanna said.

But Hanna's major contribution was to effect for the first time real organization in the Republican Party. He analyzed the political situation and decided that he could take the nomination for McKinley by winning over the delegates from the South, the Ohio Valley, and the Great Lakes region. He brought in young and talented assistants who set to work on the city, rural, and precinct level. In Chicago, for example, Charles G. Dawes was assigned to the 32nd Ward of Chicago in January 1896, enrolled immediately 1,500 young men in a McKinley club, built it up to 4,000 eager campaign workers, and succeeded in dominating the Republican district convention. Efforts to split the party at the Cleveland convention failed because Hanna would not bow to those seeking dangerous compromise. There was a bolt, but it probably helped McKinley. The day after the convention, in violation of precedent, Hanna was elected Republican National Chairman. He did not wish to waste the usual three weeks.

The organizational engine that Hanna built left the politicos panting. At the end of the campaign he had 8,000 Republican speakers in the field. Over 120 million copies of 275 different pamphlets in English, German, Italian, Polish, Yiddish, Greek, Swedish, and other languages were distributed across the nation. Both in numbers and in the quality of speakers of ability the Republicans outdistanced the Democrats in this campaign. The national committee . . . organized a body of 1,400 campaigners whose expenses were paid, and despatched them into every hamlet and country schoolhouse where there seemed to be a need.

Part of Hanna's campaign strategy was saturation bombing with campaign literature. Over a hundred million campaign leaflets were sent out from the Chicago office; twenty million left the New York office. In the massive distribution scheme, the country weeklies with a combined circulation of about a million and a half

received three and a half columns of pre-digested campaign matter a week, while other country weeklies with a circulation of a
million were given plates and mats, with appropriate cartoons, on
a weekly basis.*

Hanna ran a campaign as if it were a war. His speakers
were the troops. An intelligence service, the precursor of
today's public opinion polls, kept him constantly informed
of the shifting tides of the campaign. When his private pollsters reported that Iowa looked weak, he sent in heavy re-
inforcements. When he felt that Iowa was safe, he changed
the order of battle, redeploying his forces in Ohio, Illinois,
and Michigan. His basic strategy was built around the Midwest. Since the Republicans had no Solid South, he hoped to
weld the Midwest into a fortress. This was the beginning of
a hold on states which remained in the Republican ranks
until the New Deal shattered the conservative consensus.
When the votes were counted, McKinley had drawn mas-
sively from Ohio, Pennsylvania, Michigan, Illinois, Indiana,
New Jersey, and New York. A Republican had, for the first
time since Reconstruction, carried Kentucky. The industrial
labor vote was overwhelmingly his for two reasons:

He profited by the Cleveland depression in which 4.5 million men were thrown out of work—and by labor's revulsion
for President Cleveland's use of troops to break the Pullman
strike.

And in Mark Hanna he had as his campaign manager
someone known to be fair toward labor, though never senti-
mental. Because McKinley shared Hanna's views, it could be
said of him that "he was bound by the instinctive consistency
of his nature to represent in politics . . . the essential harmony

* Malcolm Moos, *The Republicans*. Random House, 1956.

between the interests of business and those of the whole community"—words written by Herbert Croly, Liberal editor of the *New Republic,* about Hanna.

McKinley's ability to project these views was doubly impressive at a time when the muckrakers were busily unmasking the "robber barons" and carrying on a strident campaign against capitalism. In the four years of his first Administration, labor was blessed by a surge of prosperity, business expanded, and the Midwest lost its fear of Wall Street and the East. That war came during that period did the Republicans no harm. Popular sentiment was overwhelmingly in sympathy with Cuba, Puerto Rico, and the anticolonialist fighters. McKinley sought to come to terms of moderation with the Spanish, failed, and let Congress make the initial move to war. The new sense of American destiny and the general economic well-being all worked for McKinley. The 1900 election gave him a larger share of the major party vote, or close to 55 percent. And it also brought into the Republican column six more states of the Midwest and the Pacific Northwest. Hanna's insistence that the Midwest was the core of Republicanism had paid off handsomely. Only in New England, where an influx of immigrants was changing the social complexion of the region, did McKinley lose ground to the Democrats. From that point on, the Republican hold on New England slipped in direct proportion to the increase of the Irish vote in Massachusetts and the French Canadian vote in the north of the region. Eventually, a precarious balance would be established, with victory going to the candidate—rather than the program—who appealed the most.

But Mark Hanna and McKinley could take credit for thoroughly establishing a Republican consensus which prevailed except when the party was split. It took the Great Depression,

the wizardry of Franklin D. Roosevelt, and the conversion
to Fabianism of the opinion makers to shatter that consensus.

When Theodore Roosevelt succeeded to the Presidency
after the assassination of McKinley, Hanna would mutter,
"Now look, that damned cowboy is President of the United
States." He had cause for concern. Roosevelt was a brilliant
political operator, a man of almost frightening energy, and
the first Republican to break with the concept of a Constitu-
tionally limited Presidency. He believed that the White
House should dominate the Congress and the country—that
this was manifest destiny along with America's expanding
role in world affairs. Industry had come of age, the great
fortunes had been made. Now was the time for the Federal
power to subdue them and to bring the politicians (in or out
of office) into line. Having made his reputation by extending
the scope of civil service, Roosevelt reverted cynically to a
covert reconstitution of the spoils system, thereby giving
himself the patronage of a swelling Federal bureaucracy. The
magnificent Hanna machine was scrapped—although TR
made sure that no damage was done to the Republican hold
on the voters of the Midwest, or on the machine (useful only
at convention) in the South.

It would be a mistake to think of Theodore Roosevelt during his first term as a despot or a leveler. But he believed
that "the sphere of the state's action may be vastly increased
without diminishing the happiness of the many or the few."
He honestly felt that Federal intervention could raise up the
poor without pulling down the rich, that the antitrust laws
would not be used to break up necessary industrial concentra-
tions but to increase competition. In his battles with Congress, with the "malefactors of wealth," and with former
associates, he could triumph because of his dazzling popular-

ity. For many Americans, he was not a President and a program; he was a cause, a star, a war hero, a 100 percent American who did not run from the jingoist label, a form of entertainment, and their man. No President had captured the public imagination to that time as he did. No President would until another Roosevelt began his long tenancy of the White House.

It should be noted, however, that Teddy Roosevelt's popularity would not have been so great had he not been backstopped by prosperity and a well-disciplined Republican Party whose ingrained conservatism, many felt, would act as a brake on the Rooseveltian exuberance. This was summed up by the New York *Sun,* after the 1904 conventions which gave Roosevelt the Republican nomination and Judge Alton B. Parker, a New York conservative, the Democratic designation. "We prefer the impulsive candidate of the party of conservatives," the *Sun* editorialized, "to the party which the business interests regard as permanently and dangerously impulsive." But the impulsive in Roosevelt—and his increasing acceptance of Liberal doctrine—was preparing the groundwork for his own political destruction and a bad setback for the Republican Party.

In 1904, Roosevelt handily won the election with 56.4 percent of the popular vote (7,628,461) to Judge Parker's 37.6 (5,082,754). But in the course of the campaign, Roosevelt mortgaged himself to the La Follette wing of the party, the Progressives or Insurgents. Strictly from the standpoint of party organization, this was a serious mistake for a President who had asserted, "Under no circumstances will I be a candidate for or accept another nomination." In office, he could hold the opposing factions in check. But when they met in convention, there could be no way to prevent a showdown which would be destructive to the party. The events of his times and the pressure from such brilliant but uncompromisingly doctrinaire men as Senator La Follette led Roosevelt eventually to say, "I wish to do everything in my power to make the Republican Party the party of sane, conceptive radicalism."

In 1908, however, Theodore Roosevelt still held the reins of party and country. During his tenure in office, as Herbert Agar wrote, "the nation was not divided into irreconcilable classes or regions." The school of conservatism in which he received his political upbringing still influenced his thinking. And so it was that at the 1908 convention, Roosevelt's great good friend William Howard Taft of Ohio was nominated on the first ballot by a Roosevelt steamroller whose engineer knew exactly how many votes he would poll before the delegates rose to make it unanimous. In the election, Taft won handily with more than 58 percent of the major party vote. The South excluded, the perennial William Jennings Bryan carried only three states—and these by a few thousand votes.

Taft's single term was not a joyous one. The Insurgents, unfairly attacking him as a "stand-patter," mounted an all-out offensive to which Roosevelt lent his prestige. The Congress was hostile. In the 1910 election, the strife-torn Republican Party lost control of the House in the defeat of 57 members, and it ended up with a loss of ten in the Senate. This was the *Mene, mene, tekel.* The Progressives could destroy the Republican machine but they could not build one of their own. In 1912, the split came. Taft ran as a Republican, Roosevelt under the banner of the Bull Moose and the Progressive parties, and both of them faced a fired-up Democratic Party led by Woodrow Wilson—governor of New Jersey by virtue of the demoralization of the Republican Party in 1910. It was an interesting election.

For 1912 saw the high point of organized Socialist Party strength which mobilized 901,873 votes for Eugene V. Debs. Wilson received 6,293,019 votes (42 percent) and 435 in the Electoral College; Roosevelt polled 4,119,507 votes (27 percent) and 88 in the Electoral College; and Taft drew up third with 3,484,956 votes (24 percent) and 8 in the Electoral College. A minority President—and one whose total vote was lower than Bryan's in 1908—Wilson was able to count on a majority in Congress. In 1914 he increased his lead in the Senate but slumped in the House. He was reinforced nationally by the Republican split, as well as by Theodore Roosevelt's attempts to ride conservative and Liberal horses. ("What I have advocated," he said, "is not wild radicalism. It is the wisest and highest kind of conservatism.")

In 1916 Roosevelt was still attempting to ride herd on the Republican Party, though he was not the candidate. He campaigned hard for Charles Evans Hughes, but frequently referred to him in private as "a pink-whiskered Wilson." And he took the limelight away from the Republican candidate by engaging in a massive personal battle with President Wilson. The election, nevertheless, was close, and it may have been decided by petty bickering among Republican politicians in California which caught Hughes in the middle. With 49.2 percent of the total vote, Wilson rode into office with the lowest percentage of any winning candidate since 1888. Hughes's 46 percent was the highest of any losing contender, if that was any comfort.

But for the Republican Party, it was not so grim. Though they fell seven short of recapturing the Senate, they were able to seat 216 in the House, against a Democratic 210 (with

nine independents who frequently voted with the President).
Also of comfort: The Bull Moose Party was dead and radical
Progressivism was slipping rapidly.

In 1918 the tide had already begun to turn. The Republicans polled a whopping 1,200,000 more votes in the Congressional elections than the Democrats. Wilson's reversal on
the war issue from "too proud to fight" to "make the world
safe for democracy" had been marked by the passionate support of the American people. But as World War I turned into
a frenzy of profiteering and corruption in which President
Wilson's satraps shared the taxpayers' purse, there was a
cooling down. The wave of bombings, as anarchists and their
extreme Leftist allies attempted to show their determination
to overturn the American system, made radicalism unpopular
and liberalism suspicious to the voter. The intellectuals had
other—perhaps not valid—grounds for their feelings about
Wilson. "Between Wilson and his brigades of informers,
spies, volunteer detectives, perjurers, and complaisant
judges," H. L. Mencken wrote in 1920, "and the Prohibition-
ists and their messianic delusions, the liberty of the citizen
has pretty well vanished in the United States. In two or three
years, if the thing goes on, every third American will be a
spy upon his fellow-citizens."

In short, Mr. Wilson's New Freedom turned out to be
rhetoric and the enlargement of Federal power. Seeking the
Presidency in 1920, Senator Harding of Ohio had two advantages. He looked like a President and he did not come from
the East. His call for a "return to normalcy" horrified the
sophisticated with its barbarous neologism. But it touched
a chord in the American people. "Normalcy" to them was
the quiet of the McKinley and Taft eras in which crisis was
not the order of the day every day. The shift back to con-

servatism in the nation's majority party was Harding's greatest appeal, though later writers among the "modern"
Republicans would argue that this course "imperiled the
future of the party." There is no evidence that it did.

When Harding was nominated on the tenth ballot at a
sweltering convention in Chicago, his first remark was, "I
feel like a man who goes in with a pair of eights and comes
out with aces full." He might have said the same after the
election. Though Democratic strength remained roughly
what it had been in 1916, Republican voting was close to
double. Harding polled 60.3 percent of the total vote, 63.9
percent of the two-party vote. Oklahoma and Tennessee
bolted the Democratic candidate. The Harding Senate was
made up of 59 Republicans and 37 Democrats, the House of
300 Republicans and 132 Democrats. Even the sudden and
unexplained switch to the Democrats of substantial numbers
of Negroes—traditionally Republican—failed to put a crimp
in the Harding landslide.

Warren Gamaliel Harding was by no stretch of the imagination one of the better American Presidents—although
history will rate him higher than those who limit themselves
to a contemplation of the Teapot Dome scandal which rocked
his Administration. Yet he could accomplish much quietly,
as when a letter to the head of United States Steel, Elbert H.
Gary, broke the back of the movement in the industry to
maintain the twelve-hour day. He had a simplistic view of the
Presidency which he carried too far but which should have
commended itself to some of those who followed him in the
Thirties and Forties. Calvin Coolidge, who accepted it, sum-
marized it later: "I have never felt it was my duty to attempt
to coerce Senators or Representatives, or to make reprisals.
The people sent them to Washington. I felt I had discharged

my duty when I had done the best I could with them. In this way I avoided personal opposition, which I believe was of more value to the country than to attempt to prevail by personal fear." Perhaps Harding did not realize just how much leadership was inherent in the Presidency, but he knew that the Congress was co-equal and not a perverse creation of the Founding Fathers to harass Chief Magistrates. Both Harding and Coolidge carried their respect of the Legislative Branch to extremes. The proper balance inhered in the Constitutional doctrine of conflict. As long as the battle between the two branches seesawed, deeper-thinking Presidents would have realized, the Republic was safe.

Despite his conservative view of the Presidency, Coolidge was hardly a caretaker President. On Harding's death, he took over an Administration tainted by corruption. He immediately began attacking the demoralization within the government. The men he appointed to office were all excellent choices. It has been said of him that he was "dour, reticent, and humorless," yet as Malcolm Moos added, he became "one of the most popular American Presidents." He would not be stampeded by public clamor to do something, anything, about the Teapot Dome scandal—and he renewed faith in Republican integrity by appointing a bipartisan group of the highest probity to make a legal inquiry. Then he slammed down hard on the guilty. Privately, he would say to Herbert Hoover of those who had plundered the nation: "Some people think they can escape purgatory. There are three purgatories to which people can be assigned: to be damned by one's fellows; to be damned by the courts; to be damned in the next world. I want these men to get all three without probation." Here were sentiments which washed out

of the governmental conscience less than ten years later—
and have yet to be restored.

Coolidge was clearly aware of the basic roots of his conservatism when he appointed as his personal secretary
C. Bascom Slemp, for fifteen years a Republican from Virginia's Ninth District, and a dynamo whose current continued to flow despite the concerted attacks of the Democratic
Party's biggest short-circuiters. The National Association for
the Advancement of Colored People protested mightily
against the advancement of a Southerner to a post of such
intimate contact with the President, but Coolidge held his
ground. Eventually, it was Slemp who organized the 1924
convention for Coolidge and helped pull him through to
victory despite the scandals and the postwar depression.
Coolidge, of course, proved to be a tremendous vote getter.
The "Puritan in Babylon"—William Allen White's phrase—
polled slightly more than 65 percent of the two-party vote (a
record since the War Between the States) and over 54 percent
of the total vote.

In short, the two most conservative Presidents up to that
time polled the highest percentages in the history of the
Republican Party. Coolidge was criticized, when Keynesian
economics became the vogue in the Thirties, for cutting income taxes three times yet reducing the war debt of $24 bil-
lion to $16 billion—and it has been suggested that had he kept
taxes up, it would have curtailed private spending and prevented the stock market boom. This contention is hardly
susceptible of proof. The boom was caused by years of prosperity which grew from the favorable climate for business
generated by the Coolidge Administration. A far better case
can be made for the thesis that the recession of 1929 would
not have developed into the Great Depression of the early

Thirties had economic laws rather than economic lawyers had the final say. Certainly, unemployment continued to grow under Roosevelt and even the most extravagant pump priming failed to make for more than a tiny trickle of employment. The depression would still be with us were it not for World War II. The policies generated by those who criticized Coolidge helped not at all to pull this country back on its feet.

The most notable achievement of the Coolidge Administration was the enunciation of a foreign policy which, avoiding the kind of alliances both Washington and Jefferson warned against, sought to lead the world to a Pax Americana. In the words of Secretary of State Charles Evans Hughes, this peace was to be maintained "not by arms but by mutual respect and good will." Behind this drive were Herbert Hoover, Owen D. Young, Henry Stimson, and Bernard Baruch, along with conservative trade union leaders like Samuel Gompers and Matthew Wohl. Secretary of Commerce Hoover used his office to increase foreign trade and to stimulate the exchange of goods. A "community of interests" among the Western powers, it was held, would impose order, stability, and a lasting peace. The idea was not utopian, and in the context of the American past it made sense. Had the rest of the world espoused it, history might have been different.

The Coolidge Era ended in 1927 when he said succinctly, "I do not choose to run for President in 1928." Six years later, when he died, Henry L. Mencken sweated over an obituary—as much as Mencken sweated over any piece of prose—and summed up in words heightened by his usual hyperbole. They were not precisely true, but they made sense:

The American people, though they probably do not know it, really agree with Jefferson: they believe that the least government is the best. Coolidge, whatever his faults otherwise, was at all events the complete antithesis of the bombastic pedagogue, Wilson. The itch to run things did not afflict him; he was content to let them run themselves. . . . So the normalcy that everyone longed for began to come back in his time, and if he deserved no credit for bringing it in, he at least deserved credit for not upsetting it. . . . The worst fodder for a President is not poppy and mandragora, but strychnin and adrenalin. . . . If the day ever comes when Jefferson's warnings are heeded at last, and we reduce government to its simplest terms, it may very well happen that Cal's bones now resting inconspicuously in the Vermont granite will come to be revered as those of a man who really did the nation some service.

So Mencken on Coolidge. Mencken was usually a bad prophet and a worse judge of men. But he had an affection for the offbeat—and since the press did not like Coolidge, Mencken gave him his benison. When the Hoover years began, the prognosticators looked ahead to better and greater days of prosperity. The campaign had been fought over such issues as Prohibition and Tammany Hall, with Governor Alfred E. Smith's Catholicism ricocheting among the electors and scandalizing the South. On other matters, as both admitted, there was little difference between the Republican candidate and his Democratic opponent. In the closing days, Hoover spoke up surprisingly—the issue had not really been raised—"as opposed to all forms of collectivism." His words reflected the kind of conservatism he espoused:

Every expansion of government means that government in order to protect itself from the political consequences of its errors and wrongs is driven irresistibly and without peace to greater and greater control of the nation's press and platforms. Free speech

does not live many hours after free industry and free commerce
die.

What part Catholicism and what part Prohibition played
in the 1928 campaign is still a hotly debated matter. The outpouring of votes would indicate that the nation was sorely
troubled by something. The vote was roughly twice that of
1916. Hoover, carrying 40 states (including Virginia, Florida,
Tennessee, North Carolina, and Texas), polled almost 21.4
million votes to Al Smith's 15 million. The electoral vote ran
444 to 87. The Smith campaign cut deeply into Republican
strength in New England and broke its hold on the great
cities for the first time. From the start of Hoover's term in
office, there was trouble. The Republicans had made substantial gains in House and Senate. Thirty House seats gave
the Republican Party a handy total of 267. Eight new seats
in the Senate brought the new total to 56. But this predominance was illusory. A coalition of "progressive" Republicans
and the Democratic minority immediately began to snipe at
the President and to block his legislative proposals, though
it was not until the stock market crash of 1929 that this snip-
ing from the opposition became dangerous.

The President's efforts to alleviate the financial crisis were
stymied by the coalition. In the 1930 election, the Republicans held on by a slim thread in the House—and this might
have meant the difference between action and inaction. But
before the Congress convened, enough Republicans died to
give the Democrats control. The unexpected mortality rate
destroyed all possibility that a Hoover program to meet what
was still a recession could be enacted. When Europe began
quaking, responding in part to its own situation and in part
to America's seeming bafflement, the recession became the

Great Depression. In November 1932, there were real signs of recovery—although they were ridiculed by the Democrats. But the country was shaken. The remnants of Republican Insurgency went on the war path against Hoover, and when he was nominated bolted the party. When the votes were in, Franklin D. Roosevelt—running on a platform of fiscal responsibility and a balanced budget—overturned the Republicans. He polled 22,809,638 votes to Hoover's 15,758,901—472 electoral votes to Hoover's 59. Then he sat back until March 4, 1933, ushered him into the White House.

For many who had voted for him, it was simply a change in Administrations until conditions improved. They did not know that one era had ended and another begun, that the America they had known would never be the same. The Republicans who bolted to Roosevelt were even less aware that the Great Consensus which had given the nation stability and prosperity was ended. A New Order, disguised as a New Deal in the usual game, was inaugurated with Franklin D. Roosevelt. Political forces were realigned, ideologies reshaped, ways and means revamped, and a new consensus based on the theories of the Democratic vanguard became the source of power. Instead of a majority, a congeries of minorities took hold. It would be many years before the vanquished of 1932 would think in terms of a new Republican consensus.

IV

ALMS AND *THAT MAN*— A POLITICAL REVOLUTION

When the 1932 election returns were in, Franklin Delano Roosevelt's victory might have been written off as one more instance of the pendulum swing which characterizes American politics. It had definitely been a sweep, but the Roosevelt share of the popular vote was in fact slightly lower than Hoover's had been in 1928. For the first time since the War Between the States, however, the Democrats were able to muster a majority for their candidate. But the results were not cataclysmic, and the Republicans relied on natural political forces to win back for them the Presidency and the Congress within the next four—or at most eight—years. By the old rules of politics, they should have. That 1932 marked the end of the Republican consensus which had governed the United States since 1861 was, ironically, something not even the Democrats suspected.

A good deal of rose-colored historical misrepresentation obscures the condition of the nation in those months between the conventions and the first Roosevelt Inaugural. "There is very good statistical evidence which goes to prove," Walter Lippmann has written, "that the world depression reached its lowest point in the mid-summer of 1932." And again: "Historians will see that President Hoover . . . had hold of the essence of the matter in the spring of 1932 when [he] arrested the depression." Yet the Democrats had made such a howling joke of Hoover's theme, "Prosperity is just around the corner," that the public became convinced the depression was here to stay. This, in itself, helped to wipe out the economic gains discernible in the spring and summer of 1932.

President Hoover was powerless to act. Since 1931, a Democratic House and a Senate dominated by a coalition of hostile Liberal Republicans and whooping Democrats refused to go along with his efforts to hasten recovery. After the election, Hoover might have been able to continue the upward swing. But business and public confidence drained away in the inaction imposed by the President-elect. All of Hoover's efforts to bring about some joint action in those months were rebuffed by Roosevelt. According to Raymond Moley, who at the time was very close to him, "Roosevelt felt Hoover capable of acting without his concurrence, and that until noon of March 4th it was Hoover's baby." This was smart politics but hardly responsible behavior.

By the time the 1936 election rolled around, very little had been accomplished by the New Deal, its Brain Trust, or its Congressional contingent. The Democratic legerdemain consisted of keeping voter antagonism focused on Herbert Hoover, and of occupying the eye with the flutter of alphabetic agencies, the ear with persuasive patter of the President over a hat from which no rabbit emerged. The "big" program which was to restore confidence and prove that we had nothing to fear but fear—the National Recovery Act—was such a bust that the Roosevelt Administration breathed a sigh of relief when the Supreme Court declared it unconstitutional. Public works and make work was the order of the day, but the imposition of Keynesian standards and the determination of New Deal ideologues to make business the whipping boy precluded the possibility of a real recovery. By 1936 there were still 12.5 million unemployed and some 20 million people on relief. The New Deal had already begun to crumble—and only Harry Hopkins and the billions poured into politicalized relief continued to sustain the President.

But before then, Franklin D. Roosevelt and his lieutenants had launched the political revolution which changed the face of America and introduced an ideological variant of the Marxist class struggle. What happened has been described by Raymond Moley and by others close to Roosevelt during those critical years. On the one hand, the Rexford Guy Tugwells and their socializing associates made substantial inroads into the intellectual community by their dismissal of Constitutional government as an "oxcart" in a mechanized age. Their effect on the press and the academic community was deep and lasting, serving to obscure the real nature of the Roosevelt Revolution.

Far more practical measures were being taken to ensure Roosevelt's reelection. In *The Republican Opportunity*, Moley reports that in 1935 Edward J. Flynn, the tough and efficient boss of the Bronx County Democratic machine, and Roosevelt took stock of their party and its electoral chances.

Flynn and Roosevelt noted that, except for cities controlled by Democatic organizations and the traditional Democratic system of the South, their party was nationally a rather ineffective force. They noted, too, that the Democratic Party had won the Presidency only because the great depression had temporarily upset the dominant Republican Party. . . . In 1935, Flynn spoke to me of their decision:

"There are two or three million more dedicated Republicans in the United States than there are Democrats. The population, however, is drifting into the urban areas. The election of 1932 was not normal. To remain in power we must attract some millions, perhaps seven million, who are hostile or indifferent to both parties. They believe the Republican Party to be controlled by big business and the Democratic Party by the conservative South. These millions are mostly in the cities. They include racial and religious minorities and labor people. We must attract them by radical programs of social and economic reform."

Translated into slogan form, this meant a policy of "tax and tax, spend and spend, elect and elect." Where the pattern of American electoral division had been regional and economic, it now took on a class coloration. The urban proletariat, as Marx might have put it, and the minority groups became the object of New Deal affections. Passage of the Wagner Act invested labor with tremendous power and led to the formation of the Congress of Industrial Organizations, dominated by the forces of the far Left, whether Socialist or Communist. Social Security, which Roosevelt had violently opposed, suddenly received his blessing. A systematic effort to win over the racial and religious minorities met with success. In 1936, for the first time, the Jewish vote went *en bloc* to the Democrats. The Negroes, who had—when they voted at all—usually supported the Republican Party since Reconstruction days, went almost solidly Democratic. Since more than two million Negro votes were cast, this swelled the Roosevelt total. The South, once in the driver's seat of the party, was ignored or offered a few condescending favors. Though its votes were gratefully added to the Democratic total every two years, the South was treated as the whipping boy of the city politicians and the labor leaders who now held the reins. While the American Federation of Labor followed its trade union bent, the CIO became a political arm of the New Deal.

It was in the area of "welfare" that the greatest change took place in America's political structure. Hitherto, the only group that had made a successful march on the Treasury had been the veterans of America's wars. The Roosevelt Revolution changed this, and if Harry Hopkins is to be believed, the change was a deliberate one to win votes in 1936—and in succeeding years. The statistics are corroboration. In 1935, during the pit of the depression, the United States was spending less than $7 billion for welfare programs—and of this, $2.85 billion went directly for relief. By 1962 the Federal government was spending almost $37.4 billion of which only $2.7 billion was earmarked for unemployment compensation. These figures, moreover, only tell part of the story.

To finance this expansion of welfarism, the Roosevelt Administration relied on the precedent set by one piece of legislation passed in the desperation of the Hoover Administration's waning days: the use of "back-door spending"—a method whereby Congress surrendered its control of the Federal purse strings by empowering various agencies to borrow directly from the Treasury. Though this is in direct violation of the Constitutional dictum that "no money shall be drawn from the Treasury but in consequence of appropriations made by law," back-door spending has accounted for some $115 billion since the New Deal began—or almost a third of the entire national debt.

As part of the Roosevelt-Flynn strategy for winning friends and influencing voters, the doors of the Federal establishment were thrown wide open. When Roosevelt took office, there were 588,000 people in the employ of the Executive Branch of the government. They were earning a little over

$1 billion annually. When the Democrats left office in 1952, there were 2.8 million people working for the departments and agencies of the Federal Establishment, earning more than $9.9 billion a year. The public debt was just under $19.5 billion when Roosevelt took over the Federal government. When the Democratic Party surrendered its control of the Executive Branch in 1952, the public debt had leaped to more than $259 billion.

In short, the Roosevelt Era, beginning with the enunciation of the Flynn strategy, converted both the Democratic Party and the nation to a new philosophy of government. What the liberal (and by that term, I do not mean Liberal) historian Vernon Parrington referred to as the Coercive State came into being. That Man in the White House, as the irate Republicans called Roosevelt, began by offering alms to the American people when unemployment became *his* baby, rather than President Hoover's. The coalition of a complacent South, willing to backstop the Democratic Party in elections and in Congressional jockeyings, and of a congeries of minority and special interest groups, preserved the temporary Roosevelt majority and gave it a permanence it did not really deserve. The heirs of the New Deal, in the shapes of Harry S. Truman and John F. Kennedy, were able to coast on this unlikely amalgam.

But party politics would never be the same. As a direct result of the new alignment, labor suddenly became of prime importance in electoral battles. The CIO, sparked by its extreme Leftist core, set up a Political Action Committee which was followed by the AFL's Committee on Political Education. Both these groups worked mightily to elect Democratic candidates. Not only was the prestige and power of labor leaders thrown into the scales—not to mention the labor press which thoroughly exploited its captive audience—but the Democratic Party suddenly found itself with one of the most precious election commodities. This was a disciplined, trained, and paid corps of organizers and precinct-level workers willing and able to get out the vote. In time, the labor phalanx supplanted Democratic machines throughout the country, giving the unions a hammerlock on the party.

The religious and racial aspects of the new Democratic coalition was also of significance in mobilizing the votes of people hitherto "unpoliticalized." After 1935, in the heat of the electoral contest, it became almost commonplace for the charge of "anti-Semite" or "Jim Crow" to be whispered or openly hurled at Republican candidates. The rise of Hitler which brought such suffering and tragedy to the Jews was used to inflame political passions—as late as 1952, President Harry S. Truman called General Dwight Eisenhower a proponent of the "master race theory" and in effect a Nazi. The old-time political machine, exemplified by Tammany Hall in New York City, was replaced by another kind of bloc voting. The Negro vote, the Jewish vote, the Catholic vote—all these became pawns of the men who controlled the new coalition. With almost open scorn, the pundits of the Left wrote off the Republican Party because it represented "a white, Protestant minority"—a minority, that is, when balanced against the massed and strategically placed minorities which coalesced within the Democratic Party.

In the councils of the coalition, it was assumed that nothing could break the Democratic Party's hold on the Federal Establishment just so long as tremendous pluralities could be piled up in the large cities of the population-heavy and electoral-vote-rich industrial states. So long as the South remained "solid" in Congressional (if not Presidential) elections, the coalition could weather any revolt of the suburban and rural middle classes. And so long as the Reconstruction remained a bloody rag, there seemed little fear of losing the South.

That a new coalition could form within the Republican Party never seemed to penetrate the thinking of the Democrats. Nor, for that matter, did the idea seem possible to the Republicans themselves. In election after election, they attacked Democratic strongholds where they would undoubtedly be beaten, leaving untouched naturally Republican areas which had drifted away. The Republicans, moreover, convinced themselves that to win they would have to outdo the Democrats in promises to the minorities and in offers of Federal largesse. Welfarism and the Handout State, therefore, seemed to be the program and the goal of both major parties. "Me too-ism" the popular press called the Republican line. But no matter how much hopeful Republican candidates argued that they could serve up a better Democratic stew, the voters preferred to stay with the caterers who had originated the recipe.

The 1936 election, with its vast outpouring of Federal funds, proved the shrewdness of the Roosevelt-Flynn strategy. By 1940 the outbreak of war had added another dimension to American politics. Unemployment had begun to recede markedly for the first time since the 1937 "re-recession" as a result of defense spending and the nation's military needs. But the country was divided once more on the issue of intervention versus isolationism—and here the coalition's natural sympathies were with interventionism. Roosevelt had foreseen this in 1937 and it had led him to change his own views and to ride with the tide. There was still enough conflict to allow for a change in Republican strategy. But this was not to be. Until 1962, the Republican Party's national leadership

—or, more accurately, the leadership that inheres in the Eastern Liberal wing of the party—failed to read the political signs accurately.

In the quadrennial contests, from 1940 through 1948, the Willkie-Dewey syndrome prevailed. In 1952 other factors in the political structure toppled the Democratic Party, and in 1960 a confused pattern of campaigning allowed a return of the coalition. In three elections, the Eastern Liberal wing imposed counsels of defeat on the Republican Party. The past cannot be recovered, but hindsight has its merits.

V

THE GOP AND
THE WILLKIE-DEWEY SYNDROME

The Republican Party always fared well when it was in Midwestern hands. In McKinley's day, Mark Hanna brought the party to the peak of its prestige and power. Then Theodore Roosevelt shifted its center of gravity to New York. Brilliant and dynamic, he was more for Teddy than for the GOP—and therefore willing to wreck the party machinery for causes which had little to do with the ideals and feelings of those who made up the rank and file. The Republican Party made Theodore Roosevelt, and when he broke with it, the day of victory set for him in a gaudy sunset. Those who followed him as leaders learned that lesson. Herbert Hoover had once been a Democrat, but when he joined the Republican Party, he gave it his full allegiance.

In the lean and bitter years which followed the 1932 defeat, a new spirit seized certain elements of the GOP. Though the grass-roots sentiment remained loyal to Republican traditions, there were others who wanted only to win—no matter how or with whom. They wanted to win so badly that they could taste it; and if winning meant no more than being a pale replica of the New Deal, it did not matter. It is often

71

implied that these win-at-any-cost Republicans were secretly Democratic sympathizers, that they wished to eliminate all differences between the parties because their hearts belonged to the ideological daddies of the Roosevelt program. This, obviously, is not true. Since they were, for the most part, shrewd businessmen, they would hardly have gone to the effort. Certainly, one Franklin Roosevelt would have been enough for them.

But politics is a profession. It has its rules and its values, which are seldom congruent with those of business. There have been businessmen who have made the leap into the political world, but they are not very numerous. Yet as the 1940 convention approached, it was the Eastern Liberal wing of the Republican Party—the Wall Street wing, in Populist terms—which decided to seize the reins. The toughest, shrewdest, and most ruthless political minds had masterminded the creation of the New Deal coalition. The amateurs believed that they could challenge it. It is perhaps symbolic that they chose as their candidate an even ranker tenderfoot whose offices were at 20 Pine Street—the Chase National Bank Building.

The mythology surrounding Wendell Lewis Willkie (born Lewis Wendell Willkie) would by now be monumental had he won. But even in defeat, the accounts of his rise and fall are draped with more tinsel than a Christmas tree. (A pro-Communist even wrote his life story in free verse.) The historians know that the "spontaneous" Willkie boom was contrived. They know that he was carefully selected for a particular job by would-be kingmakers who were impressed by his personality and his articulateness. But how contrived his emergence was and how his sudden appearance on the stage of history was managed are aspects of the Willkie "miracle" known only to the professional politicians and to newsmen of the times who took the trouble to find out. The strategy was simplicity itself: to eliminate Senator Robert A. Taft by spreading the word that he "can't win" and to substitute for him a candidate who "can't lose" because he can be a friend of labor and a friend of management, a liberal and a conservative, a politician and a businessman. The rank-and-file conservative Republicans would stand by him because "they have no place else to go" and the "independents" (those fey creatures who disappear into thin air just before the voting) would rally to his standard.

The kingmakers failed to realize that their logic was based on false premises. In the months before the 1940 convention, unemployment had begun to subside markedly—and for the first time without direct government subsidy. This, perhaps not so paradoxically, had awakened doubts in the minds of many as to the efficacy of Rooseveltian economics. Eight years of elixirs and panaceas which turned out to be Epsom salts had created the first stirrings of real dissatisfaction among those most prone to New Deal *cum* Keynesian thinking. The "time for a change" psychology was also beginning to peek out from under the cabbage leaf. The two-term issue and the normal nationalism of substantial numbers of Americans were also factors which would have favored a vigorous Republican candidate. The outbreak of war in Europe and the ghostly presence of catastrophe had set many Americans to thinking about the future. No time was more appropriate for raising the flag of principle.

The kingmakers never realized that if the nation wished to continue down the New Deal road, it would ride the Roosevelt bus. With an arrogance sadly mismatching their prospects, the Eastern Republican Liberals argued that they could take a man of charismatic charm like Wendell Willkie and sell him to the voters like a cake of soap. If enough people chanted "We want Willkie," it would have the desired LS/MFT effect. The candidate's job would be to lead the people into the tent; the hawkers would do the rest. This is not to say that there were no solid Republican conservatives behind Willkie. His hortatory and generalized support of free enterprise and his condemnation of the New Deal won him plaudits far beyond the value of these utterances. But as the voters discovered before the campaign had ended, Willkie was a paper tiger, constructed from leftover press releases.

In 1940, the methodology of 1944 and 1948 for barring the nomination to a conservative Republican with roots in the party was first employed. That it has not yet been discarded makes it pertinent in a contemporary context. Governor George Romney of Michigan, to take but one possibility, could be manufactured into another Willkie if the public allowed itself to be taken in once more.

The idea that the Presidential nomination was thrust upon Wendell Willkie is, of course, nonsense. Long before the public was aware of the man's existence, the idea of running for President had been suggested to him by Alfred E. Smith, financier Thomas Lamont, General Motors chairman Alfred P. Sloan, former New Deal Braintruster Raymond Moley, and others. Ernest Weir of National Steel was raising money for the Willkie candidacy prior to his emergence as a national figure. Nowhere is there a record that he discouraged this interest. As early as 1937, moreover, he had been memorialized in *Fortune* magazine which, like most of the Luce enterprises, suffers from the schizophrenia of an official editorial policy at variance with the ingrained views of its editors.

Fortune called him "the Mississippi Yankee, the clever bumpkin, the homespun, rail-splitting, cracker-barrel simplifier of national issues . . . he knows all the arguments [for free enterprise]; they are persuasive on his tongue not because they are new but because he frames them intelligently and hence makes them sound new."

But the backhanded compliment hardly stated the case. Though Willkie could talk scathingly of the New Deal, he usually found himself endorsing large portions of its practices. In the generality, he glittered. But as a putative Republican candidate he brought no joy to the professionals by attacking "the politicians of both parties" or to the voters who had sustained the GOP during the terrible years by statements that "big business is just as bad as big government." Just where he differed with the New Deal remains a moot point when some thought is given to this Willkie-ism: "Freedom is achieved by establishing certain economic guarantees. We must provide for the destitute and the unemployed; for reasonable old age pensions and unemployment allowances; for public works; for public health; for the right of labor to bargain collectively; for the regulation of public utilities and of big business."

The New Dealer might read it in one way and the free enterpriser in another. Those who promoted Willkie did not particularly care. They were interested in gathering votes. Once he was elected, these matters could be ironed out. After all, who would see the implied ideological allegiance to the Coercive State in Willkie's assertion that government—presumably the "big government" that was as bad as "big business"—"*must see to it* that the economy operates for the profit of us, the people." For Wendell Willkie, as he would admit in another context, it was all "campaign oratory." The king-

makers never learned that even in a naughty world insin-
cerity shines through. This is something the advertising
man's mind doesn't comprehend. As George Sokolsky put it,
"Those who had made the American people conscious of
body odors and the need for clean teeth believed that by
the same methods they could make the country hate Roosevelt."

The Eastern Republicans were present from the start.
But the Willkie boom did not begin to agitate the country
until such publicity men and Madison Avenue executives as
Steve Hannagan, Ted Patrick and Chester LaRoche (Young
and Rubicam), Stanley Resor (J. Walter Thompson), Fred
Smith (Selvage and Smith), and others beat the big bass
drum.* It was only then that the Eastern Liberals began their
advance on the convention. Young Governor Harold Stassen
of Minnesota who had declared for Thomas E. Dewey in De-
cember 1939—and who had also prevailed upon some of his
rich backers to supply money for the early Dewey organization—was suddenly summoned to New York by Thomas
Lamont. He returned to Minnesota a Willkie man and with
a promise that he would be made Temporary Chairman of
the convention where he would deliver the keynote speech.
That promise was kept—but Stassen's pledge to the Republican National Committee that he would remain neutral got
lost in the shuffle.

The Stassen episode was one of many. Until Willkie had
entered the lists out of patriotic duty, the chief contenders
were Dewey and Taft. Dewey was ahead in the public opinion polls and in the known number of delegates he had won

---

* Smith would later boast that "it should never be forgotten that the
'Willkie boom' was one of the best engineered jobs in history." It was notable
because in the early stages these high-powered merchandisers worked for
nothing.

in the primaries or through behind-the-scenes horse trading. Taft refused to enter the primary battles. He worked quietly with state delegations and had the support of party leaders from the grass roots up to the Republican National Committee. Had the contest been between Dewey and Taft, it is safe to say that the former would have shown more strength in the first ballot but from that point on would have slipped. Taft's advocacy of Republican principles and his unchallenged integrity would have carried the day. Of this he was confident—and so were those in the Willkie camp who knew of the powerful organization he had carefully built. It was therefore necessary to stampede the convention.

Before the convention opened, John O'Donnell and Doris Fleason, under a joint by-line, wrote that "knives flashed . . . as Wendell L. Willkie's Presidential Wall Street blitz ran into stout opposition from the embattled West." Forty Republican congressmen, mostly from the farm states, called for a "real Republican." The city slickers of the New Deal had been enough for them—and they wanted no part of a successor to Roosevelt who differed from him only in the form of his rhetoric. But while Willkie took a modest two-room suite at the Benjamin Franklin Hotel in Philadelphia to emphasize his amateur standing, a dozen headquarters for him sprang up in the city—all well-heeled and all operating at full blast. When the convention opened, the delegates were flooded with telegrams from their home states urging them to switch to Willkie. In some cases, a check proved that these wires were not sent by those who presumably signed them. Drew Pearson, who is sometimes accurate, reported that an analysis of the telegrams, though they came from all parts of the country, showed an astonishing identity in misspellings and punctuation.

Willkie was, at least, more honest than many of those who sought his nomination. Before the convention, he had told Gordon Hamilton in an interview for *Current History*, "Why should I, for the sake of conformity, catalogue myself under one of two labels when neither suits me? My political philosophy agrees with neither that of the New Deal nor that of the Republican Party as advanced by their leaders." He had boasted that he was a "La Follette liberal." He had made it clear that his Republican ties were simply a convenience. Yet with the galleries packed by enthusiasts carrying forged tickets and shouting "We want Willkie," he won the nomination. As his running mate, Senate Minority Leader Charles McNary was chosen. Frank Waldrop, in the Washington *Times Herald*, let the cat out of the bag immediately—if it was ever there:

> It is a vote-getting ticket:
> Wendell Willkie, the public-utilities president, and Charles McNary, who has pestered the New Deal into giving him a Northwestern TVA.
> And both labeled "Liberal" by traditional Republican standards . . .
> In adopting it the Grand Old Party has moved to a new base, and it will go after the New Deal on its own ground of social change.

This was precisely what the Democrats wanted. Hardly had the convention ended before Senator Scott Lucas gloated: "The majority of Republicans in Congress, including Senate Leader McNary, have been strongly against most of the policies of the Roosevelt Administration and those now advocated by Mr. Willkie. . . . They will have an opportunity to explain why, when they urge the people this fall to elect Mr. Willkie to the Presidency." The same idea was beginning to filter into the minds of the delegates, for their reaction to the Willkie nomination came amost immediately. Raymond Moley, who saw it at first hand, described it years later in his book, *27 Masters of Politics:*

Only after the noises of the convention had died away, only after delegates and party chieftains in the quiet of their homes began to unpack their suitcases stuffed with rumpled telegrams and soiled shirts, did the reality dawn. They had yielded their party to a Democrat whose political antecedents were shrouded in obscurity and doubt. They had, professionals as they were, in hot, humid haste, nominated an amateur to lead them in a desperate effort to regain their lost glory. They had gambled their all on what they regarded as a copybook statesman, inexperienced— perhaps uncontrollable.

But the worst was ahead. Willkie's first act was to propose the abolition of the party chairman—his place to be taken by a committee of five. In horror, Moley called former Republican National Chairman Will Hays, who braved a wet and stormy night to rush to Willkie's side. His answer should have been a lesson in practical politics and the way of party organization.

"There are a million little people running the Republican Party," Hays told Willkie. "Upon them depends your success. They work on the doubtful, keep the party fires going, get out the vote. They must, when they look up through the ranges of party machinery, see way up at the top a chairman they can understand. One who speaks their language, knows their needs—one who will not forget them."

Willkie abandoned the idea of his committee. But he ran the campaign according to his whims and to the advice of the amateurs who surrounded him. A young lawyer and a

Fortune magazine editor were among those who made his decisions. The shrewd Democratic boss Ed Flynn summed it up: "The organization Republicans failed to show enthusiasm. There was passive resistance." From the time of his acceptance speech, it was a steady downhill slide for Wendell Willkie. Senator Taft and Tom Dewey pledged their support and worked for him. But there is a great deal of difference between stampeding a convention and winning an election. Except for the votes he received from those who felt that his position on intervention in the war was somewhat better than Roosevelt's, he probably would have done little better than Alf Landon. The zealots who worked hard for him were never integrated into the Republican Party, and once the balloting was over, they simply slipped away. Willkie himself abandoned his post as titular head of the party and took to lecturing it. He ceased to be leader and became a critic, increasingly succumbing to the blandishments of a President who knew far better than Willkie the missed opportunities.

On the morning-after of the election, the Republican Party woke up with a colossal hangover. The candidate who was nominated because he was the only Republican who could win trailed Franklin Roosevelt by close to five million votes. In the Electoral College, the defeat was even more humiliating: Roosevelt 449, Willkie 82. Surveying the havoc they had wrought upon themselves, Republican leaders said, "Never again." But four years later—and four years after that—they succumbed to the lure of Thomas Edmund Dewey. The mixture was not quite as before, but the syndrome was the same. To make matters worse, Dewey had in the topsy-turvy fashion of contemporary politics stood the facts on their heads and decided that to win the nomination—and the election—he too must don the ill-fitting toga of Willkie Liberalism. With only a small amount of malice and some humility, the journalistic record of those zany years is appended here.

Time magazine, April 15, 1940:

Harvard History Professor Arthur M. Schlesinger [*père*], pondering the moony tides of U. S. politics, last winter came to the conclusion that sent a little wave of gloom through U. S. conservatives. His conclusion: the revolt against conservatism which began in 1931 will last until 1947–48. His qualifications: this does not necessarily mean Term III, or even continuance of the Democrats in power; but rather that no matter who is in office, the "political mood known loosely as New Dealism will govern the conduct of the government."

Why Dewey Wins, Dewey 1940 campaign booklet:

The Republican Party, wrote James McCullen in the Philadelphia *Evening Ledger,* will probably take over the Dewey strategy of accepting New Deal reforms in principle and promising to "administer them more economically and efficiently." Only a progressive Republican can win, asserted a paper on New York's Long Island, the Farmingdale *Post.* "The Old Guard will not like Dewey," predicted the Richmond *Independent* in California. . . . Many Republicans, wrote G. Gould Lincoln in the Washington *Star,* think him too liberal. . . . The Watertown, N. Y., *Times* said: "Republican chances of victory depend upon that party nominating a liberal like Dewey for the Presidency." In agricultural Minnesota, the Renville *Star Farmer* similarly declared that the Republican candidate "must be one who not only has an unblemished record of achievement, but on whom there is no taint of Old Guardism. That man is Thomas E. Dewey." *

---

* It is interesting to note that in 1939, George Gallup claimed his polls showed that the Republicans wanted new faces and a liberal program. Yet

"What's The Matter With Bob Taft?"—Alice Roosevelt Longworth in the *Saturday Evening Post*, May 4, 1940:

This technique of belittling the popular appeal of the other fellow is in full swing this year, particularly in regard to the candidacy of Senator Taft. There is general admission that he would make a good President. I have heard any number of people say, "He is just the man we would like to see in the White House," and then add, with a shade of doubt in their voices, "But can he be elected?" That question shows that the attempt to paste the non-vote-getter label on Taft has had a measure of success which the facts discredit.

The Scripps-Howard newspaper chain, June 20, 1940:

In our opinion, Willkie is the only candidate with whom the Republicans have a chance to win.

Mark Sullivan, in the Washington *Post*, June 20, 1940:

At Philadelphia, as the Republican convention gathers, they are saying Mr. Hoover would make the best President. But they say the Republicans had best refrain from nominating him because, so they say, he would not be as good a candidate as some others.

Dewey Also Ran, by Irving Stone:

The Republican convention in Chicago, which opened on June 26, 1944, was one of the coldest, dullest and most colorless in American political history. . . . The delegates' frustration was compounded of two elements: they were being used as robots to approve Tom Dewey, who had been sold to them as the only Republican with a chance to win; and they didn't believe the Republicans could win anyway. They were told that they had to

in 1960, Donald Bruce Johnson, in his *The Republican Party and Wendell Willkie* (University of Illinois Press) states categorically: "Among the Republicans at the close of 1939, there was talk of the emergence of the conservative wing from oblivion to a place of challenging dominance within the party."

nominate Dewey because the Gallup Poll had given him sixty-eight percent of the support of the Republican voters.

Gallup Poll, June 11, 1944:

If Thomas E. Dewey is nominated to run for President, he stands to win a bigger proportion of the labor union vote than any Republican candidate since 1932.

Saturday Evening Post, editorial, October 18, 1947:

It's hard work making a fascist out of an American senator who goes his way being right about a lot of things, wrong about others, sometimes ahead of his time, sometimes behind it, but all the time disarmingly indifferent to the way the things he says look in the headlines of the opposition press. . . .

If they don't want to get a Taft boom going, the gentry of the Left will do well to go back to the business of pinning wings on Henry Wallace and leave Taft alone, as union leaders in Seattle begged their followers to do. For one thing, the record shows that Taft rode into the Senate on a chorus of boos, not to mention the prediction of experts that he had made so many bobbles that he couldn't possibly get elected.*

It might be said that the 1944 election was foredoomed for the Republicans. The country was at war and President Roosevelt, as Commander in Chief, was more effective standing above the battle than if he had campaigned. It was symbolic that he delivered one of his few campaign speeches from the deck of a destroyer at the Puget Sound Navy Yard. Dewey, moreover, could not attack Roosevelt on the conduct of the war without seeming to give aid and comfort to the

---

* In 1950, the pundits predicted that in an industrial state like Ohio, Taft would be swept out of office because of his co-authorship of the Taft-Hartley Act. He won by a plurality of 437,000—the largest ever given to a Senatorial candidate in Ohio. His 1,642,537 votes topped Dewey's Ohio tally in the 1948 Presidential election by 196,853.

enemy. He was, in fact, visited by General George C. Marshall who pleaded with him on this very point. The Dewey effort of 1944 was further hampered by the chilly reaction of Republican state and county leaders who felt that once more a candidate had been thrust down their throats by the Eastern Liberal wing. They resented as well the cold efficiency of the "Dewey machine"—a group of brilliant men who seemed to lack the more human juices. Nevertheless, the trend to Republicanism continued. Roosevelt's plurality was just over 2.5 million and his percentage of the popular vote 53.8—also a drop from 1940. With a strong candidate, the Republicans felt, they could make it in 1948.

That candidate should have been Robert Taft. After his death, Walter Lippmann would write of him what many Liberals had felt all along but suppressed for partisan reasons: "The nation came to rely upon his character as something apart from his politics, and upon the quality of his mind rather than upon his political opinions. He was the very opposite of the hollow men with their prefabricated personalities. The inner man was the solidest part of Taft, and at the core he was so genuine and so just, so rational and so compassionate that he commanded the confidence of men when he could never convince them." To this extent, Lippmann was correct. Bob Taft could never convince his own party that "Mr. Republican" should be its candidate for the Presidency—or that he could and would win.

The 1948 nomination was a real prize. In 1946, on the slogan of "Had Enough?" and the general swing away from government control of the everyday economy—wage controls, price controls, rent controls—the Republican Party swept into Congress, picking up eight seats in the Senate for a total of 50, and 56 seats in the House for a total 246. This marked the highest point of Republican strength in Congress since 1928. And the man who led the Republicans in the 80th Congress was Senator Taft. Dewey, however, had sent out his team of political horse traders to sew up the nomination. He had become the hero of the Liberals by defeating Harold Stassen in a nationally broadcast debate in which the New York governor argued that the Communist Party should not be outlawed. When, on the third ballot, the convention gave Dewey the nomination, he chose as his running mate Governor Earl Warren of California—a Republican who had made a political career of refusing to help other Republican candidates.

With Warren the Vice-Presidential nominee, the Dewey campaign tone was set. Warren, before he accepted, insisted on exacting a promise from Dewey that the hottest issue of the day—and the one on which the Democrats were most vulnerable—would not be mentioned. Communist infiltration of the Federal government had filled the headlines throughout the summer. President Truman had called the shocking disclosures of Elizabeth Bentley and Whittaker Chambers a "red herring" and had moved beyond this to an excoriation of the House Un-American Activities Committee for holding the hearings which eventually brought Alger Hiss to justice and Lewisburg Penitentiary. But the Dewey-Warren ticket did not lash out at the incredibly lax standards of the Federal government, nor did it take Truman to task. Dewey was so convinced of his imminent victory that he took no precautions. In the farm belt, Dewey refused to come to grips with a major economic problem and talked of national unity.

It was the farm vote that destroyed Tom Dewey's Presidential aspirations and gave him a lower total vote than he had polled in 1944—the farm vote and the middle-class sections which had always been Republican election-day property. In both these vital areas, according to Samuel Lubell, "Truman rather than Dewey seemed the conservative candidate." And, Lubell added in his analysis of the results, "The harshest fact about the 1948 voting from the Republican viewpoint was how many ordinary conservative persons feared a Republican victory."

The lesson was clear then—and is now. For a Republican candidate to win a Presidential election, he must first be sure of the Republican and the conservative vote. Since 1940, this lesson has been forgotten by the kingmakers of the Eastern Liberal wing. Chasing a will-o'-the-wisp, they strain for a liberal effect. The labor vote which Dewey was to have gotten never materialized; those who followed the trade union leadership voted Democratic and those who wanted a conservative candidate—and there are many such in George Meany's many mansions—had no one for whom to vote. The Willkie-Dewey syndrome never elected a President, and it won't tomorrow.

VI

THE EISENHOWER-NIXON VARIANT

For the Republican Party, 1952 was the year of decision. And victory now seemed not merely a question of preference but of survival. Among the party faithful, the men and women who had by main force kept the organization alive, there was a great stirring. For the first time since 1932, the GOP was not faced by an incumbent President. Though the anti-Third Term amendment did not apply to Harry S. Truman, in principle he was excluded and so took the prohibition. While no sensible GOP politician believed that this was a "Chinaman's year" in which any Democrat could be defeated by any Republican, there was a positive sense that the long drought was about over. Long before the jungle drums began to beat along Park Avenue and Wall Street, organization Republicans had chosen their candidate: Thrice edged out by the Eastern Liberal wing, Senator Robert Taft was certain that his day had come.

But the kingmakers had also chosen their man, though with much more wisdom in 1952 than in 1940, 1944, or 1948. Like the desperate Whigs almost a century earlier, the Eastern Liberals turned to a military hero, the proportions of whose popularity they hardly suspected. They knew that the anti-Truman Democrats had in 1948 sought the hand of

General Dwight David Eisenhower and that the popular response had been good. If Eisenhower was not a Democrat, they reasoned, then obviously he was a Republican. To get him to admit that he would run, they employed a less precipitous method than the blurted love protestations of the 1948 Democratic Liberals. The troth was not plighted until the boom of "I Like Ike" sentiment had reached SHAPE headquarters in Paris and convinced General Eisenhower that he was truly the people's choice.

This is not written in irony. Eisenhower had little knowledge of politics, as he discovered once the nomination was his, and therefore could not know that candidates are only rarely not manufactured. In the political arena there is no such thing as virgin birth. Before he committed himself to the tremendous responsibilities of seeking the highest office open to an American, he wanted to be sure that he was wanted. And he wanted to be convinced that his candidacy was based on the country's need, not on factional greed. This required that the possibility of a Taft victory be made so horrendous to him that he would be forced, out of patriotic duty, to enter the lists. His reluctance to be a candidate was as soundly based as his normal eagerness to make the American Dream come true.

It is fair, I believe, to say that had General Eisenhower known the quality of Robert Taft, he would never have ventured into the Presidential arena. But as a military man, Eisenhower was suspicious of politicians and intellectuals, at ease only with businessmen. The businessman and the military leader deal in the same kind of ponderables and imponderables. The politician, and in that category I include the statesman, acts on a different kind of intuition. Senator Taft, both a politician and an intellectual, was considered dry and unemotional. This is simply a projection of the public inability to get behind the mask. No man can rise in politics without developing an understanding of the human condition. In Taft's case, moreover, his understanding was conditioned by a rigorous integrity which led him to take unpopular positions and to fight for what he thought was right even if it might have meant political suicide. Often he drove his closest friends and most passionate supporters almost to a frenzy by insisting on lending his name to dead wrong causes. He was Mr. Republican, but also Mr. Integrity. And this, specifically, was the source of his strength both in the Senate and among Ohio voters who, in large numbers, should have given their all for the AFL-CIO candidate.

In this respect, Bob Taft and Barry Goldwater have much in common. But General Eisenhower would not learn this until after the election. In the days when SHAPE headquarters was a minor Mecca for hungry kingmakers, Eisenhower was fed a strong and steady diet of "Taft is a reactionary monster" meat. All the accomplishments achieved by the blood and tears of warfare would go down the drain if the "Neanderthals" in the Republican Party—all allied to Taft— took over the government. It was the general's patriotic duty to allow his overseas cap to be tossed in the ring. Only in this manner could the nation be spared the outrageous fate of conservative Republicanism. General Eisenhower accepted what only a Superman would have doubted.

A man more experienced in politics would have wondered why these three-time losers should be so eager to return him in triumph to Washington. He would have wondered about the thousands of Republican workers who, year after year, had rung the doorbells for Eastern Liberal candidates and then wrung their hands on the first Wednesday after the first

Tuesday after the first Monday in November. Senator Taft
was their man, and triumph gurgled happily on their door-
steps like a foundling. It was a standing joke among those
who made up the Eastern Liberal wing of the party that the
Taft "troglodytes" would rather lose with their principles
than win with Ike. And to a degree there was some truth to
this. They had lost without their principles in three Presidential elections. They felt it was time for a change. If they
were going to lose, it would far more suit them to do so in
a manner which did not make the look in the morning mirror
difficult.

General Eisenhower did return, on an Eastern Liberal
wing and a prayer. But the kingmakers had miscalculated.
The Taft opposition, which should have melted under the
warm sun of the Eisenhower smile, held together far more
effectively than his best enemies would have predicted. New
and better means to blow him out of the convention were
needed. There could be no voices from the sewer (that was
Democratic stunting) and no packed galleries chanting his
name. A gimmick will work only once. A flood of telegrams,
such as those which inundated the Philadelphia convention
in 1940, would be discovered for what it was. After all, Senator Taft's followers were not going to be stung twice. They
were, in fact, ready to act quickly to expose any fraud. But
they could not foresee that the man most known for honor
and integrity in the American political firmament would be
driven from the nomination by the broadcast admonition,
"Thou Shalt Not Steal." It is not necessary to rehearse here
the Great Delegate Steal which was perpetrated behind that
pious slogan. As Representative Carroll Reece said after
Eisenhower's maiden political speech, "It looks like he's
pretty much for mother, home, and heaven"—and against

any stealing by anybody except Henry Cabot Lodge, Jr., and Thomas E. Dewey who were managing the campaign.

When the convention delegates began marching on Chicago, Taft led with 530 delegates out of 1206; Eisenhower had 427. There were 118 uncommitted and a scattering of the rest, with Governor Earl Warren clinging to 76 and waiting for the *coup de grâce* from Nixon which would throw him out of contention. (Those who wept over this perfidy had never seen the scars on Nixon's back—the result of knife wounds inflicted by Warren in the 1946 and 1950 campaigns.) To the delegates, Eisenhower was represented solely as the candidate who could win. The Eastern wing of the party was, as usual, filling the news columns and the airwaves with predictions that Taft couldn't win. Impossible, the pundits said, impossible. Taft, on the other hand, continued to argue his conservative program, to note the Democratic record in China and Korea, and the bankruptcy of the Welfarist-Coercive policies at home. The delegates preferred his words to the gentle platitudes of Eisenhower's speech writers.

The "Thou Shalt Not Steal" propaganda, spelled out in publicity releases and in printed leaflets slipped under the door of every delegate, brought in the Madison Avenue dimension. Those entrusted with the task of selecting a Presidential nominee suddenly felt that the eyes of Moses were upon them. And the Eisenhower managers whispered that delegates who stuck to their guns would be marked for life. Worse still, they would be choosing a man who could no longer command the respect of the millions of "independents" waiting in the wings for their quadrennial courtesy— followed by refreshments at the Democratic table. The issue, however, was hardly so simple, and the Eisenhower position hardly so moral, as the huff-and-puff brigade argued. At question were the delegations from Texas and other states, all pro-Taft, and rump delegates from those states who asked to be seated and argued their spurious legitimacy.

At previous conventions, delegates whose seats were being contested could vote on the credentials of other state delegations but not on those of their own. The Eisenhower forces, however, insisted that wherever there was a contest, the delegates could not vote on any credentials. The effect of this procedure would have bogged the convention down—for any group of disgruntled Republicans could have challenged their state delegation and thereby effectively spiked its guns. The parliamentary aspects of the fight are far too complex for this account. There are, however, two points to make: (1) By accusing Taft of vote fraud, the Eisenhower forces were able to win the battle and seat their own delegates; and (2) at the same time, they guaranteed a split within the party which was not healed until 1962. Senator Everett M. Dirksen, rising to his greatest rhetorical heights, told the convention as he pointed at Governor Thomas E. Dewey, the New York delegates, and the assorted kingmakers: "We followed you before and you took us down the path of defeat." The response of the delegates and the galleries to this thrust told the story.

That Dwight David Eisenhower won the nomination and swept into the White House is history. Those who laid their all on the altar of his election found themselves in the months and years carrying their heads tucked neatly under their arms. Senator Henry Cabot Lodge, Jr., General Eisenhower's aide-de-camp in the campaign, was defeated in his own bid for reelection. Others, as the years went by, learned that the paths of other men's glory led but to a political grave for them. And the question was never answered: Who was responsible for Eisenhower's victory? Certainly, he was popular as a war hero. But the very pro-Ike Scripps-Howard papers were, in anguish, warning editorially that his campaign was "running like a dry creek." There are some today who feel that what saved the Eisenhower candidacy was the incredibly stupidity of the Democrats in raising the Nixon "secret fund" issue and Nixon's success in turning the sword back on his attackers.

None of this matters very much. What counted then—and to this day rankles—was the manner in which the Eisenhower Administration systematically alienated the Republican organization and favored Liberal Democrats when the patronage plums were being picked. It was a standing joke among Republicans during the Eisenhower years that the best way *not* to get a job in Washington (qualifications being equal) was to be known as a card-carrying member of the Republican Party. It is but a small and sad commentary that the first Eisenhower Fellowship, supported by private funds contributed by Treasury Secretary George Humphrey and other businessmen, went to Douglas Cater, a staff member of the then firmly Liberal publication, *The Reporter*. Other far more important jobs were snatched from hard-working Republicans who, in 1961, moaned and groaned when the Kennedy Administration began consolidating its power by applying a spoils system which would have gladdened the heart and inspired the admiration of Andrew Jackson.

That Republicans did not gather the rosebuds of political victory was one verse of the sad song. Other aspects of the Eisenhower years were far more damaging—and galling. The President of the United States is at once the Chief Magistrate and his party's leader. Eisenhower, to be blunt about it, had a concept of the role which had gone out with the more naïve civics textbooks in the nineteenth century. The President saw himself as above party, and so he grimly rejected the hard work of rebuilding an organization that had fallen apart during the years of Democratic hegemony. Organization is not quite the proper word. A political party, if it is to be successful, is an organism which must be nourished and exercised. If it is simply an organization—that is, a collection of individuals harnessed to the same machine—it cannot function properly in that most touchy of human operations, a popular election. It cannot make itself heard or reach the quick of the body politic. An organism must have a brain and a heart as well as legs and arms and a voice. Years in which the kingmakers had presumably supplied that head and that heart left the Republican Party somehow disjointed.

President Eisenhower thought of the Republican Party as an army which could, with proper fire power and logistical support and given the proper training, win battles. An army must also have the will to win, as General Eisenhower should have known, but his two terms of office robbed the Republican Party of that inner *raison d'être*. It takes hardly any perceptiveness to discover the reasons for Eisenhower's defeats in the by-elections, his inability to elect a Congress—all at a time when his popularity was very high. In the 1952 sweep, the Republicans captured the Congress—and then promptly lost it in 1954. To the horror of party leaders, they failed to recapture House or Senate in 1956, and so for six of the eight Eisenhower years the Congress was in Democratic hands. After every defeat, Vice-President Nixon got together with Victor Johnson, the GOP's congressional campign expert, to plan a strategy for victory. But Nixon was not President. Lacking the adhesive of patronage and the prestige of the White House, he could only make the state and county chairmen aware that there was at least one person in Washington who thought about them.

The sole effort by President Eisenhower to revitalize the party was his ritualistic lip service to "modern Republicanism" and his call to the "progressives" to get behind the GOP. The net effect of this was to create dissension in the ranks. The Liberal wing of the party, which had not been able to deliver the cities but had sufficient success to have loud support in Congress, assumed that this was the signal to declare war on the conservatives. The conservatives, who make up the greater part of the party and hold most echelons of the party hierarchy, felt that they were being disowned. There was almost an inverse ratio to the size of Eisenhower's popular appeal and the morale of the party he presumably led. A cynical observer might have supposed that these slighting references to Republican conservatives were with malice aforethought designed to drive them out. And to a degree this was true for some of the more doctrinaire Liberals within the party. Only by the dissolution of the unhappy union, they hoped, would the Grand Old Party move on to victory as the Grand New Party.

Eight years of Eisenhower in the White House left the party dispirited and still hoping that his coattails would somehow materialize and become a flying carpet. The work and determination needed to rebuild the Republican Party were not to be found. The new recruits who could have sparked the engine were never solicited. Increasingly, they came of their own accord, as the conservative movement began reaching into the nation's campuses and seizing the imagination of young men and women who wanted more from their country—and from their government—than bread, circuses, and cradle-to-grave swaddling clothes.

This was the party Richard Nixon inherited. His opportunity was great and the prize was almost in his reach. Yet he missed because his confidence in the conservative principles which monitored his early career had been shattered by the men who became his associates in the Vice-Presidential years. No party can have too many practical politicians, but not at its head. Nixon's personal convictions remained conservative. But he had been conditioned to believe that a conservative "can't win." He did not carry this idea to the illogical conclusion that only a Liberal can win; in the name of practicality, he tried to bridge the gap between the Left and Right of the GOP, and thereby proved himself the most impractical of all. The GOP gap is unbridgeable in those terms. Had Nixon been stronger—and less subverted by the Eastern Liberal and kingmaker wing—he would have left his calling card at the houses of the Liberals and greeted them with a warm smile on the street, but his own primary attachment to the Taft-Knowland forces would never have been questioned.

The kingmakers had winged Nixon once when they tried to prevail on General Eisenhower to drop his running mate during the 1952 "secret fund" episode. They had winged him even more seriously in 1955 when they talked Eisenhower into proposing that Nixon withdraw from the 1956 race and accept a Cabinet post. Eisenhower did his best to shame Nixon into this withdrawal. From that point on, Nixon felt that he must keep his left flank protected by making a deal with the Liberals. And so, before the Presidential race had even begun, just before he left for Chicago and the 1960 convention, Nixon shot himself in the foot by "coming to terms" with Nelson Rockefeller. Nixon gained nothing by this meeting. But the Republican Party faithful saw it as a sign that the mixture would be as before. Forgotten was much in the Nixon record which might have reassured them. All that remained was the recollection of words and deeds said and committed when he was the official apologist for the Eisenhower Administration—a position he could not avoid.

Nixon also accepted the formulation that a Republican could win only by gathering to himself large numbers of Democratic votes. To this there was more than a little truth— but only if the proposition were carefully examined and explained. By seeking Liberal Democratic votes, a Republican Presidential candidate merely lost Republican votes and gained nothing. Liberal Democratic votes were not up for grabs; but many conservative Democrats, deprived of their franchise within their own party, looked wistfully in all directions for a candidate who would share their thinking. To the bitter end, Nixon thought he would make inroads into the Democratic vote among minority groups. He counted on the fact that, working behind the scenes and without any pressures, he had accomplished much for Negroes. He had, moreover, a far better civil rights record than Senator John F. Kennedy. But the Negro leaders who had repeatedly assured Nixon of their undying devotion twitched not a muscle for him—and told their followers to pull the lever or make the cross mark for Kennedy.

There is no doubt that Nixon was deprived of the Presidency by massive vote frauds in Illinois, Missouri, and Texas. In some Southern districts, almost twice the eligible vote cast itself for Kennedy, thereby overcoming a Nixon lead. But the truth of the matter was and is that Nixon should have won so big that no amount of stolen votes could have prevailed against him. The margin of defeat was in the Republican precinct workers who had little heart for what they suspected would be another eight years of disaffection at the White House. The precinct workers and the state Republican officialdom went through the motions. But their worst fears seemed to be confirmed by the candidate. Acting as his own campaign manager, Nixon had little time for demonstrating his capacities as party leader. He isolated himself from those whose good will and shoe leather were so vitally needed. Lacking the Eisenhower charm which could burst through to every man in a crowd, Nixon did not substitute the show of interest—and in a good candidate that interest is real, no matter how bone-tired he is—which is the mark of a good political leader. He cut his campaign to the Willkie-Dewey pattern in one respect: More Republican leaders were mad at him on election day than right after the convention. This should have been the tip-off.

Richard Nixon lost by a margin of 112,000 votes. A shift of 90,000 votes in four states would have given him the election. The fineness of the margin was doubly heartbreaking, for Republican muscle dented precedent by snatching 21 seats in the House of Representatives from the Democrats. Was there a moral in this? Indeed there was—that hybrids make good corn but bad candidates, that Republicans like to feel they are voting for Republicans, that conservatives are getting somewhat testy at being confronted every four years with a candidate chosen by the kingmakers and fashioned to a Liberal image. The 1960 election, however, laid the groundwork for 1962 and 1964 by demonstrating to the Republican Party that even a candidate of limited popularity, surrounded by controversy and running a bad campaign, could come within an inch of victory. The question then and now was this: Who has the prerequisites for victory? Who is the "can't win" candidate, the Liberal or the conservative?

The party workers had their answers. It was, they felt, a matter of imposing their answers on those who every four years stormed the Republican convention and ran off with the candidate. Fortunately, with every passing day, the alternatives became clearer. If the kingmakers succeeded in their quadrennial snatch, no one would be able to say that the delegates had not been warned.

And if the kingmakers had any new hopes, they could paste in their crowns the words of the Washington *Star*'s David S. Broder:

"Even in victory . . . the professional politicians are of two minds about such men-above-party [as Eisenhower]. They admired General Eisenhower for the quality of leadership he gave the nation. But they felt a certain regret, shall we say, that when he left office, the Republicans had only one-third of the governors, one-third of the senators, one-third of the representatives, and one almost-but-not-quite-elected President."

VII

WINDS FROM SOUTH AND WEST— THE NEW ALIGNMENT

The Gallup pollster wanders about the country asking his question: "Suppose the Presidential election were being held today. If Rockefeller and Goldwater were nominated for President and Vice-President on the Republican ticket and Kennedy and Johnson on the Democratic ticket, which ticket would you like to see win?" Dr. George Gallup must know what is wrong with that question, but in mid-1963 he still published his results: Kennedy-Johnson 56 percent, Rockefeller-Goldwater 38 percent. And the headlines were written: JFK SLATE BEATS TOP GOP PAIR. Even if the sampling was a good one and the "factors" worked into the Gallup blender in order to arrive at a "proper" mix were not whimsical, the question proved nothing except that President Kennedy could beat Governor Nelson Rockefeller—and it has never required a poll to determine that.

The Gallup question was mischievous in dragging the Goldwater name in as Vice-Presidential choice. The man in the second spot can occasionally lose votes for the Presidential nominee as Senator Henry Cabot Lodge, Jr., hurt Richard Nixon. But only on very rare occasions does the second man's popularity rub off on the first. The man who is polled simply thinks of a Kennedy versus Rockefeller race and expresses himself accordingly. Dr. Gallup, or if not he any mildly competent politician, also knows that when an incumbent is pitted against individuals who are not even candidates yet, he always comes out ahead. Polls are worth very little, and even less than that before the two parties in convention assembled have chosen up sides.

"Mischievous" is the word, because the polls have come to be used not to gauge public opinion but to form it. And the Gallup Poll, by the weighting it admittedly does (and by its subjective approach) has tended over the years to raise clouds of dust, blinding people into acting according to what in this day of non-books might be called non-knowledge. A change, at first subtle and now there for all to see, has been taking place in the nature of American politics and in those alignments which control elections. States and regions once safely Democratic are swinging to the Republicans, and vice versa. The "marginal" district, a term applied by the professionals when the winning candidate has less than 55 percent of the vote, is becoming more the rule than the exception. None of this is reflected by the pollsters who are still wondering how a state like Maine can bring such confusion to the pundits.

Whether or not President Kennedy wins in 1964, the country is up for grabs to the party and the party leaders who come forward with programs which the people want. The day of the safe election is rapidly passing, and it is a question whether it will ever return.

The new alignment is motivated by a variety of factors. One, which the Liberal strategists have not yet realized, accounts for their present dominance in the Democratic Party and the national life. Even before the Great Depression, hundreds of thousands of young men with political ambition turned to the Democratic Party. Dissatisfaction was a small factor, but more important was this key fact: The Republican Party was in. It had long since filled the posts. Its leaders were entrenched and had no intention of stepping down for young pretenders. The Democratic Party was wide open and begging for help. When Franklin Delano Roosevelt elbowed Al Smith out of the nomination and then successfully stormed Washington, the New Deal opened its arms and its purse to hordes of the young and middle-young who immediately moved into the old and new Federal agencies and proceeded to dig in.

In the 1960s, a young man with drive and political aspirations knows that he is not going to replace Arthur Schlesinger, Jr., or McGeorge Bundy. The saplings planted in Washington by the New Deal have grown strong roots. In the party framework, it is a long struggle to rise to the level of men who sit at the top of the ladder. If the young would-be politician or candidate comes from the South, he will turn to the Republican Party because the openings are there. It is a brand-new party that is coming into being on the other side of Mr. Mason's and Mr. Dixon's line. It is also a rapidly expanding party. Given the temperament and the drive, the sky's the limit. (And the vista is wide: There has not been a Southern President since the War Between the States.) The same applies to the Rocky Mountain states and to the Pacific Northwest. And it is doubly true in the big cities.

Take New York City. There has not been a real Republican Party in Manhattan and the Bronx in living memory. Until recently, certain districts were owned lock and stock by Tammany Hall—and the Republicans went home in a barrel after every election. It is a matter of history that after the unexpected Republican Congressional sweep in 1946, a so-called Republican leader explained to Democratic boss of the Bronx Ed Flynn that he had nothing to do with electing a Republican congressman from that burgeoning borough. Flynn was gracious about it; he knew it was true. Those who would make politics their career or their avocation expect nothing from the Democratic clubhouses. But since there is no regular GOP organization to speak of, they know that if they are willing to start from the bottom, much can be achieved. The political effect of this can be graphically demonstrated by comparing a Young Republican and a Young Democrat meeting.

But the new alignment, while it applies to changes in regional voting patterns, in the emergence of the big-city suburb as an area of conservative Republican strength, and in a shift in the political balance of power which will make it increasingly difficult for Democrats to claim majority status, is also psychological. There may be reverses in the future, but an objective sampling of sentiment indicates that the demonstrations and the excitement over conservatives like Barry Goldwater are the surface manifestation of a deeply running current in American life. This may be forgotten in the echo chambers of propaganda which deafen the voters before every election with Liberal slogans. But the mass rejection by the wheat farmers in 1963 of the Administration's $2-a-bushel handcuffs—a triumph of sense over the handout—cannot be underestimated. In increasing numbers the voters are getting ready to shoot Santa Claus because they have discovered that while he talks of Christmas goodies he is picking their pockets. What is happening can be seen in the strength shown by an infant Conservative Party in New York. With

inadequate funds and battling electoral laws which discrimi-
nate against new parties, it got itself on the ballot and polled
close to 150,000 votes.

The optimism which the Goldwater forces in the Republican Party began feeling in the spring and summer of 1963
could be traced to a reading of these signs. But they were
inspired as well by two facts: (1) Senator Goldwater is "Mr.
Conservative" and will appeal both to those who demand a
Right-Left confrontation and to those who are tired of the
eeny-meeny-miny-mo method of candidate selection; (2) he
is a Republican who will run as a Republican rather than
spend his time trying to wash himself clean of the party label.
Apologetic Republicans may occasionally win, but they do
nothing for their party. Previous experience has made the
GOP more than impatient of those who talk Republican only
until they have the nomination in their hands. But beyond
these intangibles of human reaction, there were other and
firmer causes for optimism.

There was, to begin with, the South. Only the bitter mem-
ories of the Reconstruction had solidified the South into a
monolithic Democratic block. And when the fragmentation
seemed imminent, along came the depression and a New Deal
whose blandishments in that pitiful time were well-nigh impossible to overlook. Federal patronage, as dispensed by the
free-spending Treasury, did the rest—and if it came from
what most Southerners considered a bunch of radical dam-
yankees, at least they were Democrats. To complete the
New/Fair Deal hold on the South, there was the question of
seniority in Congress. Southern legislators in House and
Senate, coming from safe constituencies, were able to be returned to office repeatedly. This gave them the chairmanships
of key committees. The Warren Supreme Court probably

had more to do with the resurgence of two-party feeling in the South than any other single factor.

In part, this was due to the startlingly sociological decision in *Brown vs. the Board of Education*. But basically, the cause went far deeper than the civil rights issue or the integration controversy. In decision after decision, the Supreme Court showed such a marked contempt for the will of Congress and all legal precedent that thoughtful Southerners began to realize their committee chairmanships availed them nothing. Only by massed political power could the conservative South make its mood felt—and such a demonstration was impossible within the Democratic Party. Southerners who got their political indoctrination and information from sources other than stump speakers also saw that with the rapid destruction of the States' Rights concept, the Federal government was centralized to a degree hitherto considered inconceivable. At the same time, they watched the abuse of the Federal power and the slow erosion of those unique features of the American system which had made this country prosper. As Liberal economic policies slowed down the nation, prosperity turned one corner while the New Frontier turned another. Almost abruptly, many Southerners realized their kinship with Northern conservatives. The New Deal had introduced class-war concepts into American politics, and suddenly millions of people discovered that they were looking down the barrel of a gun.

It was, then, the realization that fiscal and economic principles are irrevocably connected with political principles which aroused a South until then in the long-distance thrall of Northern Democratic politicians. And with this, there was a corollary realization: The South's Democratic congressmen were guaranteeing the success of New Frontier programs by

going down the line for President Kennedy. In test vote after
test vote—when the GOP held the line—it was the Southern
contingent in the House of Representatives which provided
the Administration with its margin of victory. On civil rights
matters, the delegations from the various states of the old
Confederacy held the fort. But on other legislation, they fled
like raw recruits when the Democratic leadership swung into
action. A survey made by the *Congressional Quarterly* showed
that the much-vaunted "conservative coalition" was all too
often coalescing elsewhere. It made its will felt in only 14
percent of Congressional roll calls. Southern Democrats supported the Kennedy Klub on 86 percent of his program when
it came for a vote.*

The 1962 election was the first real sign that the South
had indeed risen again—peacefully, but cognizant that the
only instrumentality left to conservatives was the Republican
Party and aware that an investment in it was the surest guarantee against that "opening to the Left" which the kingmakers
had always sought in the past. But 1962 was only a start. The
pundits and their cousins had smugly predicted that this was
a flash in the pan—the last feverish heartbeat of a dying party.
But the trend continued into 1963, as M. Stanton Evans, the
brilliant young editor of the Indianapolis *News,* reported:

In February, a Goldwater Republican was elected to the
Georgia state senate, and another to the Mississippi House of
Representatives. In March, St. Petersburg, Florida, elected a Re-
publican mayor. In April, two Republicans were elected to the

---

* "Only on two key votes in two and a half years, where we were totally
committed and had to fight, have we lost on a measure to a combination of
solid Republican vote and a significant Southern Democratic defection," a
Kennedy Congressional liaison man has said. A majority of Southern congressmen even supported Kennedy on the packing of the Rules Committee,
thereby weakening their own hold on House machinery.

City Council in North Augusta, South Carolina. In May, the citizens of High Point, North Carolina, gave Republicans a clean sweep in their city elections. Several Republicans now sit in the Texas legislature, the latest addition being a representative from once-solidly Democratic Corpus Christi. Another Republican recently won election to the Fort Worth City Council. The mayor of Mobile, Alabama, is now a Republican—and, in fact, the Republican senatorial candidate last year carried every major city in Alabama.

The "several Republicans" in the Texas legislature numbered eight. To the list could be added three Republican mayors in North Carolina, another Republican mayor in Fort Worth, Texas, and the defeat (also in Texas) of a five-term Liberal Democrat by a Goldwater Republican in a special election for a seat in the legislature. Defections from the Democratic Party were celebrated at "Resignation Rallies" in Texas. Fifty Democratic precinct leaders resigned in a body at one such meeting.

This phenomenon caused editors and wire services to send their Washington correspondents South to beat the bushes and to determine the truth or falsity of reports that the old monolith was a thing of the past. Jack Steele, a Scripps-Howard reporter who cannot be accused of being soft on conservatism, was one of those who made the voyage of discovery. "The Republican Party—driven by a powerful crew of young, aggressive leaders—is gaining support and muscle in Dixie much faster than anyone would have dared predict a year ago," he wrote in June of 1963. And GOP strength, he added, "could swing a majority of the South's electoral votes to the GOP next year—if anyone except New York's Governor Nelson Rockefeller is the party's nominee."

Being a good reporter, Steele noted that Republican leaders in the South "are trying to build their party's base on 'conservatism' . . . as a counterpart to what they regard as the Democratic Party's 'radicalism.' In many states including the Carolinas and Alabama, the GOP has party organizations which already outstrip those of the Democrats. They have set up active state, county, and even precinct committees and are training thousands of doorbell-ringers and poll-watchers. The Democrats, who have never had or needed such party machinery in most of Dixie, now are trying belatedly to catch up." And, Steele added:

These GOP organizations already have brought party victories in scattered Congressional, legislative, city, and county races. And their power is concentrated in cities and industrial centers which produce heavy votes—in contrast to the GOP's weakness in northern urban areas. Such local Republican triumphs seem sure to be extended to statewide races for governorships and United States Senate seats in the Deep South in the next year or two.

If there was any proof needed of these observations, it could be found on Capitol Hill. The Southern delegation to the House, which had been convinced that there was no percentage in maintaining any coalition with the Republicans, suddenly turned cozy. Democratic Congressmen whose basic sympathies and thinking were conservative and Republican quietly began an investigation of the possibility of changing their party designation. Dangerous as this would be, some felt, it might be less perilous than retaining the Democratic label. Many voters in the South made it clear that they wanted no part of any futile "third party" movements—unless the Republican candidate turned out to be someone punched out by the same cookie cutter that produced Wendell Willkie and the other "sure winners."

It takes Americans eighteen months to choose a President and a year to get over the election. From the moment that the lines were drawn, the South made it clear that it wanted no substitutes. Republicans predicted that a Liberal candidate heading the GOP ticket would wreck all chances of building a strong and permanent party in the South. Democrats agreed that only a conservative trusted by the voters of the South could carry the region. And both had one candidate: Senator Goldwater. It was not only his political philosophy, not only his personality, but the sheer irritation felt by Southerners at what they considered the cynical game of musical chairs which the Eastern kingmakers played with them—the kingmakers of both parties, who usually turned out to be the same group.

The surveys bore out the predictions of the politicians. Repeatedly it was demonstrated that President Kennedy's popularity had taken a bad nose dive in territory Democrats had once considered their private domain. How far that toboggan slide took the President, the polls showed only to a limited extent; the pollsters always hedge their bets. But there was, from the middle of 1963 on, general agreement that Kennedy could no longer take for granted 50 percent of the voters. Unless a crisis bigger than those perceived by the Chicken Littles of Washington descends on the nation, the condition will continue to prevail. Of the thirteen Southern states (including Oklahoma and Kentucky which some categorize as Border) only Arkansas remains precarious in the Kennedy column—and its six electoral votes are not causing any great rejoicing at 1600 Pennsylvania Avenue. Georgia

was considered doubtful, but the combination of Goldwater
and conservative sentiment seems to be increasing. Louisiana,
some of the smart money says, can go either way. All the rest
seem locked in the Goldwater embrace. As the Shreveport,
Louisiana, *Times* commented:

Virtually every GOP candidate elected at Southern state and
Federal levels in the past year ran as a "Goldwater Republican"
as opposed to a Kennedy Democrat, with segregation raised
neither pro nor con on either side. With neither pro nor con dis-
cussion from us as to Mr. Goldwater, the fact remains that it is
his breed of conservatism and not merely the GOP label that
caught the fancy of at least a couple of million or so one-time one-
party Southern Democrats as they went to the polls in 1962. . . .

But the South is only part of the picture. Kennedy won
with most of the South and the big industrial states. Could
he do it with the big-city vote alone? The answer, to many
experts, has seemed a flat No. And even these states are in
some jeopardy. With the death of Robert Taft, Ohio fell
upon Democratic days, but now it seems safely in the Republican column. Kennedy carried Illinois by a small squeak and
the padded Cook County vote. Last year's mayoralty election
in Chicago though won by the Democrats, kicked the stuffing
out of any hope that Cook County could deliver again. This
time, the GOP will have its poll watchers out to see that the
vote is counted properly. The downstate rural conservatives,
many of whom sat on their hands when Nixon was the candidate, are expected to add to the Republican plurality—if
Goldwater is the candidate.

California remains in the doubtful column, but the picture has been increasingly bright. After the 1962 gubernatorial election, the Republican Party was in bad shape. The

Nixon candidacy had left the party torn asunder—and the defeat healed no wounds. But in the months that followed, former Senator William F. Knowland began edging back into politics, drawing the pieces of California's Republicanism together. The departure of Nixon for New York's greener pastures helped; with him present, the party would have remained divided. Most encouraging was the surprise victory of Del Clawson in the 23rd Congressional District of Los Angeles. In a special election, he reversed a onetime 2-to-1 Democratic lead to a 5–3 Republican conservative win. All labor's horses and all labor's men worked to stop Clawson, and failed.

For Kennedy, there remain New York, Pennsylvania, New Jersey, Massachusetts, Connecticut, Rhode Island, and West Virginia in the East. Goldwater Republicans are ready to concede these states. They are ready to concede Michigan, Minnesota, and Missouri as well—though the breakup of the Walter Reuther-United Auto Workers machine in Michigan may bring some surprises in 1964. Oregon and Nevada are also considered by some a safe bet for Kennedy. All the rest the Goldwater forces claim. Based on these figures, *U. S. News & World Report* could say in April of 1963 that it was possible for Goldwater to carry the nation by 280 electoral votes even if all the states marked uncertain in the surveys went to Kennedy. This would leave the President 196 electoral votes. As one political observer has said: "The only thing Kennedy seems to have going for him is the fact that Presidents usually get reelected. But is that enough?"

Another recent survey offers this analysis of Goldwater's prospects for 1964. The figures in parentheses are GOP votes in the 1960 campaign.

THE SOUTH

GOLDWATER	vs.	KENNEDY	ROCKEFELLER	vs.	KENNEDY
Alabama—10 (42.2)					Alabama—10
		Arkansas—5 (43.1)			Arkansas—5
Florida—14 (51.5)					Florida—14
		Georgia—12 (37.4)			Georgia—12
Louisiana—10 (49.6*)					Louisiana—10
Mississippi—7 (63.7*)					Mississippi**
North Carolina—13 (47.9)					North Carolina—13
South Carolina—8 (48.8)					South Carolina—8
Texas—25 (48.5)					Texas—25
Virginia—12 (52.4)					Virginia—12

TOTALS Goldwater 99, Kennedy 17; Rockefeller 0, Kennedy 109

NEW ENGLAND

GOLDWATER	vs.	KENNEDY	ROCKEFELLER	vs.	KENNEDY
Maine—4 (57)			Maine—4		
New Hampshire—4 (53.4)			New Hampshire—4		
Vermont—3 (58.7)			Vermont—3		
		Massachusetts—14 (39.6)			Massachusetts—14
		Rhode Island—4 (36.3)			Rhode Island—4
		Connecticut—8 (46.3)			Connecticut—8

TOTALS Goldwater 11, Kennedy 26; Rockefeller 11, Kennedy 26

* Figures for Louisiana and Mississippi include States' Rights vote.
** If Rockefeller is the Republican nominee Mississippi will probably vote for a slate of independent electors, as it did in 1960.

GOLDWATER	vs.	KENNEDY	ROCKEFELLER	vs.	KENNEDY
		THE FAR WEST			
Oregon—6	(52.6)	California—40 (50.1)	Oregon—6		California—40
		Washington—9 (50.7)			Washington—9
		Hawaii—4 (50)			Hawaii—4
		Alaska—3			Alaska—3
TOTALS Goldwater 6, Kennedy 56;			Rockefeller 6, Kennedy 56		
		BORDER STATES			
Kentucky—9	(53.6)	Missouri—12 (49.7)	Kentucky—9		Missouri—12
Oklahoma—8	(59.0)	West Virginia—7 (47.3)			Oklahoma—8
Tennessee—11	(52.9)		Tennessee—11		West Virginia—7
TOTALS Goldwater 28, Kennedy 19;			Rockefeller 20, Kennedy 27		
		THE EAST COAST			
		New York—43 (47.3)	New Jersey—17		New York—43
		New Jersey—17 (49.2)			Pennsylvania—29
		Pennsylvania—29 (48.7)			Maryland—10
		Maryland—10 (46.4)			Delaware—3*
		Delaware—3 (49.0)			
TOTALS Goldwater 0, Kennedy 99;			Rockefeller 17, Kennedy 82		

* Delaware repeatedly elects a conservative Republican Senator, John Williams, but has a checkered history in Presidential elections. It is therefore rated a tossup for both Goldwater and Rockefeller.

GOLDWATER	vs.	KENNEDY	ROCKEFELLER	vs.	KENNEDY
THE MIDWEST					
Illinois—26 (49.8)					Illinois—26
Indiana—13 (55.0)			Indiana—13		
Wisconsin—12 (51.8)		Michigan—21 (48.8)	Wisconsin—12		Michigan—21
Ohio—26 (53.3)		Minnesota—10 (49.1)	Ohio—26		Minnesota—10
TOTALS Goldwater 77, Kennedy 31;			Rockefeller 51, Kennedy 57		
THE PLAINS STATES					
Iowa—9 (56.7)			Iowa—9		
North Dakota—4 (55.4)			North Dakota—4		
South Dakota—4 (58.3)			South Dakota—4		
Kansas—7 (60.4)			Kansas—7		
Nebraska—5 (62.1)			Nebraska—5		
TOTALS Goldwater 29, Kennedy 0;			Rockefeller 29, Kennedy 0		
THE ROCKIES					
Montana—4 (51.1)					Montana—4
Idaho—4 (53.8)			Idaho—4		
Colorado—6 (54.6)			Colorado—6		
Utah—4 (54.8)			Utah—4		
Wyoming—3 (55.0)					Wyoming—3
Nevada—3 (48.8)					Nevada—3
Arizona—5 (55.5)			Arizona—5		
New Mexico—4 (49.4)					New Mexico—4
TOTALS Goldwater 33, Kennedy 0;			Rockefeller 19, Kennedy 14		
GRAND TOTALS Goldwater 284, Kennedy 248;			Rockefeller 153, Kennedy 371		

Any tabulation of a future vote is, of course, foolhardy. But if used as a guide it explains why a supporter of the "draft Goldwater" movement told *U. S. News:*

There are three varieties of Republicans: the hard core conservatives; the conservatives who think the party cannot win with a conservative nominee, and the liberals. Usually, at a convention, the liberals and the second group are in control. But the first two groups could control things just as well. If there is a candidate who all the conservatives think can win, then there will be a different picture at the 1964 convention from what we have seen in the past.

The most cogent argument to support the contention that Goldwater can win whereas Rockefeller cannot is based on an analysis of candidate strength in an Electoral College rather than in a Gallup Poll context. The Rockefeller strength is concentrated in areas where Kennedy is stronger. Where Kennedy is weak, as in the South and the Midwest, Rockefeller is weaker. The Goldwater forces have not sought to find a candidate and a program that in Stanton Evans's formulation "appeal to a mythical average person of the Gallup Poll findings. It depends upon choosing a candidate and a program that appeal to majorities in a constellation of states adding up to a majority in the Electoral College."

If the Republican Party ceases to act as if national elections were national plebiscites, if it seeks out those to whom its program and candidate are intrinsically appealing, and if it focuses its campaigning on areas of probability rather than on those of impossibility, it will win. This is the Goldwater strategy. It is a sound one, though many party leaders, bemused by the humanitarian smile and the steely eye of the kingmaker, have forgotten it. Early in the campaign, *News-*

week and *Congressional Quarterly* discovered that most Republicans favored Goldwater but many felt that he would be deprived of the nomination by the Eastern Liberal cabal. This kind of thinking, *Newsweek* remarked, "is so widespread it suggests to some political observers that deep-dyed Goldwater supporters don't know their own strength—and, as they discover it, they will be less and less willing to settle for any other candidate."

They discovered it when an Atlanta *Constitution* poll showed that in the summer of 1963 Goldwater would have gotten 250 of the South's 305 convention votes—with his stock still on the ascendant. They discovered it again when leaders of 23 states with 209 electoral votes said Goldwater would run better than Rockefeller, whereas in only 14 states, with 196 electoral votes, did Rockefeller run ahead. These signs have accumulated. What few have pointed out is that a Goldwater candidacy would combine the outburst of enthusiasm which marked the first days of the Willkie campaign with the steady and vital push of the party workers, from precinct level up. This is what wins election. And this is what makes a political organism of a party organization.

VIII

BIG CITIES, THE LABOR VOTE, AND A MYTHOLOGY

In October of 1962, Barry Goldwater spoke his mind to the editors of *U. S. News & World Report*. What he had to say was in part prophetic, in part didactic. As a Republican—and the chairman of his party's Senate Campaign Committee—and as the undisputed leader and spokesman of American conservatism, he had at once to be teacher and leader. In the informal manner which so maddens those who wish to color him dull, Goldwater expressed himself on the Republican problem in the big cities. His documentation was sound, but significantly it was not this but his broad approach which got to the nub.

He was asked: *The Democrats get the labor unions and minorities in the big cities, don't they? Do the Republicans have an answer to that?*

"Yes," said Goldwater, "I think we have to go to work. For so long we've just said, 'We can't do it, we aren't going to get the labor vote.' Well, that's a lot of poppycock. Forty-two percent of organized labor are Republicans. At least, a number of studies show that."

Q. You mean a union member isn't always a Democrat?

A. No. And if you go after them, you'll get them. In my own state, we are as heavily unionized as the national average, or approximately so. I think we're one percentage point off. My biggest pluralities come out of the most heavily organized districts—because I go after them. . . .

Q. What appeal gets across to them?

A. Just talk with them. They're not interested in Taft-Hartley. They're not even interested too much in their own unions, the great majority of them. They're interested in the same things that you are. I guess I talked to at least 10,000 workers in the last campaign, and just once did the subject of labor law come up. The shop steward was a man I went through kindergarten and grammar school with. We sat down on the floor in the mill and ate lunch. And he said, "Would you explain to these fellows 14b of the Taft-Hartley Act?" That's the only time anything about labor came up.

Now, generally, the Republican approach is, "Well, I haven't a chance with them, so I'm not going to talk with them." Or, when a Republican goes to talk with them, he has a well-prepared speech about what's wrong with the Taft-Hartley Act. Now you can't find me many labor leaders that know anything about the Taft-Hartley Act, let alone labor members. They just want to know what's happening to the country and the world.

They're interested in taxes. This is the group that I call the "new capitalists." They're actually making more money than they need to live on. They own stock. . . . They own small properties.

So the Republicans should go after these people. We're not going to get 53 percent of them, but we might get 45 percent instead of 42 percent, as at present.

Senator Goldwater's remarks were just a once-over-lightly on the question of the big-city and labor vote. So too were his comments on organization and the Democrats. "Frankly, I don't think you find many Democratic organizations except, well, in Massachusetts—the Kennedy outfit—New York City, which is a combination of 'liberal' and Democrat, and Mayor Daley's outfit in Chicago. . . . I think Kennedy is making the same mistake that the Republicans have made ever since 1928, when they placed all the marbles in the President's basket." What Barry Goldwater had to say could be documented in a serious and revealing study completed by Ohio State Chairman Ray Bliss at the behest of the Republican National Committee. Bliss was asked to make a survey in depth to determine why Richard Nixon lost in 1960. Being a technician in politics, he did a remarkable job of pulling all the facts together and arriving at objective conclusions. No matter how much a politician wants to win with his candidate, he is a fool if he closes his eyes to the facts and the reactions of those who, in the long run, are the final arbiters. The Bliss study and its corollaries indicated beyond doubt that the GOP lost the big cities because of apathy and pessimism. If this is a harsh judgment, it can be sustained by the record. The bad Republican showing can be justified on ideological grounds only to a very limited extent.

The key fact in assessing Republican strength in the big cities and among trade union members is that it becomes available when the candidate seeks it—much as Barry Goldwater said. Senator Taft had no difficulty in carrying the large urban centers of Ohio; and in 1950, with all the big Democratic guns from President Truman down campaigning against him, Richard Nixon polled the largest vote of any candidate running for the Senate in that year, even though he defended Taft-Hartley. Barry Goldwater's strength in Arizona's urban centers did not derive simply because he talked to union members. Talking is not enough; it depends on what you say. And Taft, the younger Nixon, and Gold-water talked the kind of sense which can reach labor groups. What they said inspired confidence—and nothing can replace this as a vote getter and a vote holder. Only the most doctrinaire will put union above country. Only the most narrow-minded can fail to see that self-interest requires an understanding of all economic factors. The successful candidate brings the economic issues home not by uplifting sermons on the virtues of the free enterprise system but by frank explanations of how it benefits all in an open society.

(Senator Goldwater once described to this writer why those who worked for his family's businesses supported him politically. "When we embark on a new policy, we explain just why we do and how it will benefit everyone in the company by increasing our profits. And anyone, no matter what his job, is entitled to examine the company books to find out if we are telling the truth." This is sound politics and good economic education. All the class-conscious propaganda in the world cannot compete with this kind of honesty.)

On January 12, 1962, Ray Bliss demonstrated to the Republican National Committee just why the GOP did so badly in the cities. Like all great truths, what he said was very simple. Said Bliss:

"A questionnaire was sent to forty-one cities with population of over 300,000, excluding Washington, D. C. Thirty-four of the forty-one cities replied. The replies disclosed that the Republican Party has only thirty-seven full-time paid people working in local party headquarters in twenty-five major cities to promote the party's cause among more than 25 million people. Only fourteen of the forty-one cities produced Republican majorities in 1960, and five of the fourteen were in the deep South. This certainly indicates a pitiful lack of adequate staffing in most of the big cities, and obviously leaves the Republican leaders in those cities at a considerable disadvantage in competing with the highly efficient COPE-Democrat operation." COPE is the Committee on Political Education, the AFL-CIO's heavily financed political arm. "In my preliminary report made last June," Bliss continued, "I stated that a survey of scattered heavily Republican precincts in several large cities where we lost showed that an average of better than one hundred persons, who said that they were Republican-minded, either were not registered or did not vote in the 1960 election."

Obviously, no party wins which does not get out its vote. And the vote stays home unless there is adequate staff to register the potential voter and then get him to the polls. Thirty-seven people entrusted with the job of mobilizing 25 million people is somewhat disproportionate. The Democratic Party has its paid staff in the organizers and officials of the AFL-CIO. The Republican Party, lacking this machine, must count on volunteer help. This help has come from the conservatives in the party. But in the past elections, conservative Republicans have been offered candidates who have tended to gloss over the differences between Democrat and Republican, Liberal and conservative. Republican candidates, obsessed by the idea that they must appeal to the urban voter, have attempted to carry the big cities. But as the shrewdest GOP strategists have pointed out, it is not necessary to carry these cities—simply to reduce the Democratic margin to the point that Republican strength in the suburbs and the rural areas can compensate for the discipline of the COPE-Democratic machine.

The 1960 statistics tell the story:

In Michigan, Nixon took 70 of the state's 80 counties and

came down to the Detroit city line with a majority of 244,880. But Kennedy piled up a 311,721 margin in the city, carrying the state by 66,000 votes.

In Illinois, the GOP piled up a 447,454 plurality outside of Chicago. But because the Republicans failed to guard their flank in Chicago, the Daley machine was able to claim a Kennedy plurality of 456,312 votes. Nixon lost the state's 27 electoral votes by 8,858 votes—a negligible number when the ballot boxes are stuffed.

In Pennsylvania, the Nixon margin was 215,228 outside of Philadelphia. A well-oiled COPE machine with Democratic boss Bill Green at the wheel gave Kennedy a winning plurality of 331,554 Philadelphia votes—and another 32 electoral votes. A shift of five thousand votes in St. Louis would have given the Republican Party the Missouri electoral vote. And Republican precinct workers at their jobs would have brought in more than that number, preventing as well the theft of many thousands of more votes. As Bliss pointed out, moreover, "in 1960 Nixon received 33.4 percent of the [St. Louis] vote. In 1961, under vigorous leadership, the Republican candidate received 37 percent of the vote. If Nixon had received this percentage, he would have carried Missouri. What helped make the difference? In 1960, only 486 of St. Louis's 786 precincts were staffed by Republican workers. In the race for mayor, 636 of the 786 precincts were staffed by Republican workers."

Elections are won by organization. Yet in 34 big cities surveyed by the Republican National Committee, it was discovered that only two had a full-time paid chairman to run a campaign. Only 18 cities had a full-time paid executive officer of any kind. Only six of the cities could boast of a full-time public relations director and only four others had a part-time publicity man. Three cities were able to report that they had a full-time finance officer, two others had a part-time finance official. Only two cities had a full-time organizational chairman and only one other had a part-time official doing precinct work.

This situation led Senator Gordon Allott to remark that "the Republican Party is losing literally millions of votes purely by default, and most of these are concentrated in the cities." The wonder is not that the Republican Party has not carried the big cities but that it has done as well as it has. With no organizational structure, with a substantial number of precincts ignored (even on election day), with no publicity and no financial director, any Republican vote becomes a gift and little else. The GOP, moreover, must cope with COPE *and* the Democratic Party. The Philadelphia Story of 1960, as described by Senator Allott, gives a good picture of the COPE operation:

COPE began a registration drive in January 1960 by successfully urging Mayor Dilworth to form the so-called Mayor's Non-Partisan Registration Committee. A mammoth advertising and publicity campaign was launched.

Radio, TV, newspapers, billboards, posters, civic club forums all were used. In-plant registration was approved. The Mayor sent a registration letter home through 250,000 school children. It was all wonderfully civic. Nobody could be against it. As usual, COPE and its friends were the most active, while Republicans relied largely on the innate—and inert—instincts of the good citizen.

A barrage of mail containing registration promotion and guidance went from COPE headquarters to local unions. The locals placed the names of all members on 3-by-5 cards, which COPE divided by wards and divisions. These were checked by COPE

workers against registration lists. Locals were instructed to register
those members not registered.

A final week was set aside for a special effort. Wives of union
members undertook Operation Bus Party, touring housing proj-
ects to register voters. COPE provided transportation and baby
sitters to those desiring to register. The municipal workers union
and the city administration called on all city employees to ring
doorbells seeking registration.

There was a parade; a citizenship day rally; special programs
for senior citizens. Finally there was Operation Saturation in
which sound trucks toured working class areas and paid COPE
workers combed door to door.

There is nothing reprehensible about this. COPE did its
job, getting 176,532 new voters registered. The Republican
Party did not try to counter this push for Democratic votes.
It merely complained—and hoped. But this was only the first
step for the labor forces. Local unions supplied 6,000 poll
workers and ordered 5,000 union members to make 25 phone
calls each for the Democratic candidates. Half a million
copies of so-called voting records of the candidates it favored
were printed and distributed at COPE's expense. Three-
quarters of a million copies of an anti-Republican tabloid
newspaper were handed out. Pocket cards, campaign kits,
pictures of Kennedy, and other sundry electioneering devices
were distributed by COPE.

On a nationwide basis, 40 million pieces of literature were
printed and sent out by COPE—at the expense of all AFL-
CIO members, even those who favored Nixon. Every major
city in the country received copies of 122 ten-second TV spot
announcements. For radio, 456 different platters containing
recorded political commercials went to big-city stations. Some
630,000 posters went to local and state COPE headquarters.

More than a million supervised phone calls were made by the Women's Activities Division, which was broken up into 440 units. The entire professional staff of many local unions was put at the disposal of Democratic candidates. Most important of all, COPE's effort was on a year-round basis. The Republicans, on the other hand, forgot all about the labor vote until after the campaign began. A whirlwind courtship and love at first sight may be convincing on a half-hour television show, but in politics they seldom come to pass.

The sad, sad fact of big-city voting is that the Republican Party expects its principles to win the voter. But the voter must be told, and in this the GOP has been signally bashful. It has even failed to reach out to one portion of the urban electorate which is just as important (though not as numerous) as the labor vote. The middle-class community has been left alone in areas of great Democratic strength, as if anyone with an income in excess of $10,000 were a political Typhoid Mary. In most sections of Manhattan, for example, registered Republican voters can go for years without getting so much as a postcard from their party or in support of its candidate. In some sections, it is difficult to find out who the candidate is—so that in Congressional elections, the GOP gets only the determined straight-party vote. Though millionaires cleave unabashedly to the Democratic Party, Republicans have shuddered at the charge that they are the "party of business" —in effect accepting the Fabian views of their critics. "Big business," fearful of the Justice Department's Antitrust Division, has limited its contributions to money which it frequently distributes on a bipartisan basis.

It can be stated as a general truth that if the Republican Party put one-half the effort now expended in wooing the unwooable minority to the recruitment of middle-class voters, and if the middle-class voter put one-half the effort now expended on community fund drives into political organization, the "big-city problem" would disappear. The GOP would get those extra percentage points which mean the difference between victory and defeat on the statewide (and the Electoral College) level. This was demonstrated conclusively in the germinal 1962 election. Preachments from party leaders are not enough. It requires hard work and the kind of determination which restored Ohio to traditional Republican hands. Unfortunately, far too many GOP state organizations are as convinced that they can do nothing in the cities as the national organization once was that efforts in the South were a waste of time and money.

The pundits have, of course, given wide currency to the idea that Republican success in the cities is an impossibility. They have now given it a new shine by "explaining" that the Republican opening in the South will antagonize Northern voters in the urban areas. They therefore create a false either/or dilemma for the GOP. But the Democratic Party has thrived by parlaying a strong Negro and civil rights vote with that of the rural Southerners. The simple fact is that in many Northern cities, a Republican organization exists only on paper in the Negro districts. It used to be said that the Puerto Rican vote was "solidly" Democratic until Luis Ferré, head of the Republican and Statehood parties on the island, campaigned actively in New York, Philadelphia and other cities where *puertorriqueños* live. An example of what hard work and shrewd campaigning can do may be found in New York's East Harlem where for years Representative Vito Marcantonio won reelection to the House. Marcantonio was a Communist in a district made up predominantly of Italians. The Communist Party had no strength there, but he was able to win his primary battles in the Democratic and Republican parties from his base of operations in the splinter (and pro-Communist) American Labor Party. The voters in the district did not care whether or not Marcantonio was a Red. They knew that they could go to him with their problems. Eventually, it took a combined Democratic-Republican effort to dislodge him. During this period, Negroes who saw no hope for advancement in the Tammany-run Democratic organization looked in vain for GOP precinct and district workers or a full-time clubhouse where they might get to know the local leaders.

The organizational efforts invested in the big cities will be wasted if the Republican Party attempts to follow the Liberal road. For the most part, those few Republicans who have succeeded in large Northern urban centers have built up a personal machine which has collapsed when they moved on to greener pastures. This certainly was the case in the Washington Heights district of Jacob Javits when he gave up his seat in the House to run for the Senate in New York. The only steady source of manpower and enthusiasm is the conservatives who work through Young Republican groups or in Young Americans for Freedom. It is these young conservatives who pack the Goldwater rallies and who have already begun to infuse new life in moribund Republican organizations. If the GOP allows itself to be led down the Liberal garden path, it can never hope to build again the kind of party groupings which once projected and elected the great figures in the industrial states who rose to national prominence.

If the 1964 election does not bring victory to the Republican Party, the choice of the candidate will determine whether it can survive and grow or decline into petulant desuetude.

Destroying the mythology of "inevitable Republican failure" in the big cities will be an important step in avoiding that fate.

New forces are at work to advance the Republicans in the cities which are nullifying the power of the bosses. Rowland Evans and Robert Novak, writing in the New York *Herald Tribune,* noted them:

The big city bosses, whose political muscle powered John F. Kennedy to the Presidency in 1960, might repel more voters than they round up for the President in the 1964 election.

This is neither the wishful thinking of Republicans nor the nightmare of starry-eyed reformers. It is the private assessment of hard-headed Democrats who believe the Kennedy political high command is playing with dynamite in keeping intimate ties with machine politicians.

Recent years have produced abundant evidence of the vincibility of the Democratic machines.

The Philadelphia machine made a pitiful showing in renominating Mayor James Tate against poorly organized reform opposition. The Baltimore machine was routed by a patchwork reform ticket. Mayor Richard Daley of Chicago was elected to a third term, but by a surprisingly small margin over a nondescript Republican opponent.

But the diminished ability of the machines to deliver the vote within the city limits is only part of their trouble. Ever since the war, the Democratic city has been lagging behind the Republican suburbs in growth—sometimes even losing population. The city vote is becoming less important every election.

Moreover, the noxious quality of the machine bosses becomes more intense the longer the distance from their center of power.

In 1964, many Americans will only have to go as far as the polling booth to get away from this center of power.

IX

ROCKEFELLER—FRONT-RUNNER
TOO SOON?

Mr. Walter Lippmann is frank, if nothing else. In the April 1, 1963 issue of *Newsweek,* Lippmann wrote on "Rockefeller and the GOP"—and it is doubtful that the Governor of New York will ever forgive him for it. In the clearest of language, the eminent columnist committed the sin of saying too soon what Nelson Rockefeller would not have wanted broadcast until he was safely ensconced in the White House. The Lippmann column merits extensive quotation:

Unless all the signs fail, the Republicans are once again going to justify the words of Mr. Dooley when he said of the two Presidential candidates that they were as far apart as the two poles and as much alike. Barring miracles and accidents they are going to nominate Nelson Rockefeller to oppose John F. Kennedy. This will give the country a choice *(sic)* between two enlightened conservatives who have received their enlightenment from the same economic and social textbooks. On the central issue of how America should be governed in this century, their differences can be detected only by reading the fine print.

The Lippmann column noted with cold truth that over the years the Republican Party had chosen candidates "who under somewhat different circumstances might have run on the Democratic ticket." He suggested that it might be good, just to clear the air, for a man of Senator Goldwater's "antique conservatism" to oppose the "modern conservatism" of President Kennedy. And then he got to the nub of the question:

As a candidate, Governor Rockefeller's best hope would lie in the claim that while he and Mr. Kennedy have much the same doctrine and policy of economic growth and social welfare, he can do better than Mr. Kennedy in inducing Congress and the country to accept the program. . . . Rockefeller's credentials are first rate. Indeed the Kennedy domestic program is based on the same philosophy as the reports of the Rockefeller Brothers' Fund. Both go back to the pioneering works of the great modern economists, notably Wickell and Cassel in Sweden and John Maynard Keynes. The Rockefeller reports were the first popularization of the new doctrine.

As the high priest of contemporary Liberalism, Lippmann was delighted at the thought that no matter how the voters jumped, the man in the White House would change domestic and economic policies hardly a jot. Kennedy or Rockefeller, it was all the same—and under those circumstances, the nation could hardly be expected to buy Brand X when the name brand was up for sale by the Democratic National Committee. These observations, however, appeared in print when Nelson Rockefeller was trying desperately to remake his image, thereby hoping to appeal to the GOP's rank and file and to the state and county leaders in the Midwest and the South who, presumably, would then turn away from Senator Goldwater and respond to him. Having, when he ran for Governor of New York in 1958, received the endorsement of the ultra-Liberal New York *Post*, Rockefeller had reversed his field. In 1963, conservatism was fashionable, and the great Rockefeller brain trust was advising that any "opening to the Left" be saved for post-election festivities.

The Lippmann crystal ball turned out to be cloudy on Rockefeller's chances. True, no one but die-hard supporters of Barry Goldwater believed at the time that any candidate other than Rockefeller could even come close to the Republican nomination. It was signed and sealed; the delivery would in time follow. In New York, however, a head of steam was building up which blew the safety valve even before Rockefeller's remarriage to Margaretta "Happy" Murphy had seriously compromised his chances for the Presidency. For one thing, the conservatives were in no forgiving mood in the spring of 1963. When Rockefeller seemed to be on top of the world—back in May of 1962—he had spoken out too flippantly about the people whose support he would need to get the nomination, and against their heroes. Of Barry Goldwater, he had said: "He's attractive, articulate, courageous—and wrong." The conservatives he had backhanded with, "These right-wing groups are like cattle that aren't going anywhere. They're scared and they'll fly off in any direction."

The new conservative stance fooled no one, least of all the correspondents who covered him. On a disastrous trip to Washington, right after the Lippmann accolade, he had turned sharply on Kennedy, and in the shock James Reston, the *New York Times* Washington Bureau chief, had given him the unkindest cut of all, in any Liberal context. "Nelson Rockefeller was in Washington this week, but his old friends scarcely recognized him," Reston wrote. "He talked like Harold Stassen and acted like Dick Nixon." That Rockefeller winced is understandable. Stassen has become a symbol of utter futility among Republicans and Democrats alike. Nixon remains anathema to the "old friends" mentioned by Reston. But Reston piled it on by adding, "He has about as much chance of losing the nomination as he has of going broke, but he is denying everything, wooing the conservatives, and assuming that this is the traditional road to glory."

The rhetoric is confused, but the point is clear.

The Reston obituary for Rockefeller's character must be read against a background of events in New York State. The *Wall Street Journal* had been saying that "bothersome home-state problems are clouding" the Rockefeller Presidential horizon. Scandal and public indignation were on the rise. Pro-Rockefeller members of the state government were frankly admitting that they did not believe he could be re-elected governor. Corruption involving his State Chairman L. Judson Morhouse and the State Liquor Authority would have filled the dailies were it not for what his aides considered the providential newspaper strike. Morhouse, who doubled as the chairman of the New York State Thruway Authority, was called before a grand jury. His refusal to waive immunity and his resignation under fire did Governor Rockefeller little good; he had been one of those closest to Rockefeller in the political maneuvering that led to victory against Democratic Governor Averell Harriman. The *Wall Street Journal* quoted a "lukewarm Rockefeller Republican" as having said, "I don't think disclosures will be sufficiently wicked to dent his Boy-Scout image"—which is about as luke-warm as you can get without freezing to death. Governor Rockefeller was not touched by the scandal, but a procession of others in his administration were. Clean as a hound's tooth though he might be, the Liquor Authority disclosures did little to enhance Rockefeller's argument that in the White House he could do it better.

The citizenry was also up in arms over Governor Rockefeller's attempts to increase taxes in his home state. This opposition is fairly unusual for New Yorkers, who have developed a numbness in the pocketbook nerve. The Internal Revenue Service takes its bite of income, the state follows on its heels, and the city has found new and ingenious ways to abstract its share. The outrage was not over the proposed increase in auto and liquor taxes but in the fact that the Governor had flatly promised during the 1962 campaign that there would be no further surgery on the voters in the form of new taxes. The citizenry, cynical though it may have become, considered the proposed new taxes dirty pool. In many Republican communities, the town fathers passed resolutions condemning Rockefeller. Newspaper editorials were not kind. Legislative mail was heavy and nasty. Bumper stickers warning DON'T STEP ON ME blossomed on the highways. And the neighborhood cocktail lounges and saloons announced a "Rockefeller cocktail—same old ingredients, just add 15 percent to the price."

That there may have been a valid reason for the tax did not involve the general reaction. Nor could Nelson Rockefeller understand why the citizens opposed what he considered necessary—which automatically made it right. This is part of the Rockefeller character, and in public office character can sometimes be more important than ideology. Character, however, does not simply involve the honesty, devotion to duty, personal loyalty, and all the virtues or lack of them that are employed in measuring a person. How a man works and what he feels about himself are part of his character. How he responds to crisis is another. Whether he will gamble for big or little stakes—or not at all—is a third. In the context of this kind of character, Stewart Alsop offered a brief anecdotal view of the man in *Nixon and Rockefeller: A Double Portrait* published by Doubleday in 1960:

Here is an anti-Rockefellerite who saw Rockefeller in action in Eisenhower's Washington: "Because Nelson's never had to worry about money, he has no real idea of its value. And he's just as extravagant with people as he is with money. He had something like eighty people working for him in that cold-war adviser's job —Bill Jackson, who succeeded him, found there wasn't enough work for half a dozen. The budget and the bureaucracy would both get out of hand if he ever became President."

Even some who know him well and admire him have their private doubts about a Rockefeller Presidency. "Nelson has only one fault, but it's a serious one," says one friend. "He has no real critical faculty. I've seen him rubbing his hands with enthusiasm over half a dozen wild-eyed schemes. In the White House, that could be a dangerous business."

Another, and closer, friend has this to say: "Nelson's one great weakness is that, because of his circumstances, he has never known *real* pain, *real* suffering, *real* defeat. As a result, his world is an unreal world, a lopsided world. He is the embodiment of the great American illusion that all problems are soluble, that if you devote enough brain power and enough money to a problem, you always come up with an answer. He does not realize that there are problems which have no answer, and that worries me when I think he might be President."

If these are Rockefeller's friends, he has no need of enemies. But there is considerable truth in what they say, and the public subconsciously realizes it. He is, in a sense, an unreal man, a human front for a UNIVAC machine or the guardian of a mechanical brain trust. The public sees his smile and feels his handshake. But the warmth is very temporary. Those who have worked for him—what Alsop calls his "princely retinue"—are always aware that their right to a seat near the throne can at any time be withdrawn. In his relationships with those who work for him, Rockefeller is much like Franklin Delano Roosevelt—something that all his biographers have noted. Rockefeller admired the second Roosevelt and has tried consciously to emulate him. He believes that by keeping his brain trusters on the edge of their chairs, he improves their efficiency. And, like Roosevelt, he deliberately fosters conflict among them, hoping that from it will emerge constructive action. Several people are simultaneously given the same assignment—something that improves neither their sleep nor their disposition—and it becomes a case of Devil take the hindmost.

There is one great difference. Roosevelt took his ideas from all about him, then used the brain trust to develop them and to find ways to make them palatable to the public. Rockefeller's brain trust is the seedbed. The beautiful round fruit is produced by the congeries of thinkers, economists, publicists, writers, and experts he keeps on the New York payroll or borrows from the multitudinous Rockefeller philanthropic and business enterprises. When he moved into the Governor's Mansion in Albany, Rockefeller had under his arm 134 studies on how to improve the state government. The brains and the computers had done a fine analytical job. Unfortunately, politics is not an exact science and government is even less well defined. There are too many imponderables, and the winds of public opinion tend to blow the blueprint into the swamp.

That Rockefeller can be the prisoner of his research was no more dramatically demonstrated than at Glacier National Park, Montana, on June 28, 1960, when he lectured the annual Governors Conference. Rockefeller was justifiably concerned about the state of the nation's defenses. The Rockefeller Brothers' Fund had prepared one of its inevitable studies for him. On this he based his conclusions, though in his speech he sought to rest them on his experiences in the Federal government under President Eisenhower. His use of private information and research therefore had a kind of imprimatur; he seemed to be talking for the Administration, which he was not. (What he had to say was known to be in-accurate by the Pentagon and the White House.) Since then, the true state of affairs has become public knowledge—but during the 1960 campaign the Rockefeller analysis was used with telling effect by Senator John F. Kennedy as the "proof" for a contention that a "missile gap" existed. The Rockefeller estimate of United States strength almost sounds like a Ken-nedy speech. Said Rockefeller:

The basic facts are these:

1. In the years 1961 to 1964, the Soviet Union will have more long-range missiles than America. And the number of our own retaliatory missiles will be inadequate.

2. . . . In the event of a surprise attack, only a small percentage of our [long-range bombers] could ever leave the ground.

In point of fact, the United States was at the time not only ahead of the Soviet Union in missile power but also extend-ing that lead to the point where, by 1963, some within the Administration were urging a cutback in production to pre-vent too much "overkill." The nation's long-range bomber force, under the Strategic Air Command, was on 24-hour alert, with a classified number of planes always in the air. SAC, moreover, was the world's most powerful and most combat-ready offensive force in history. Still relying on his own "whiz kids," Rockefeller stated that "modern nuclear weapons, with modern means of delivery, mean that a surprise attack could, in itself, be decisive. . . . Thus in [a] few minutes, the inadequately defended country can lose its effective retaliatory power, lose half its population, and fall at the aggressor's mercy. . . . We have serious limiting factors in the ability of any of our surviving retaliatory forces to strike back after attack." Without tremendous expenditures, the situation would get worse rather than better, he predicted. This, of course, has not been true—and the vast expenditures of the Kennedy Administration have not contributed markedly to what was a continuing upsurge in American military strength until Defense Secretary Robert McNamara began slicing up the military with his slide rule.

Because Nelson Rockefeller is, by the sometimes unconsciously revealing testimony of friends and observers, a product of his brain trust, he can look bad one day and good the next. Similarly, he can also be the closest thing to a political chameleon this country has seen. When he worked as Roosevelt's director of the Office of Inter-American Affairs, Rockefeller was, to quote *The Progressive*, "not then much different, to all appearances, from any other bright young New Dealer." When in June of 1962 he made a swing through the Midwest, he talked so convincingly of free enterprise and individual initiative that he left his audiences temporarily certain that they were seeing a "new Rockefeller." In his utterances on foreign policy, he berated President Kennedy on Cuba in terms which could have come from a "hard" anti-Communist. Yet on another occasion, he switched over to the one-world concept so dear to the heart of Wendell Willkie. (Like Willkie, he likes to say that "big government is as bad as big business.") The answer to the world's problems, he asserted, "is some free-world, supranational political being with the power to tax, especially for aid for under-developed countries, public health, and roads." Since the United Nations is rapidly moving in that direction, any Rockefeller Administration would presumably urge it along.

Who are the men who give Rockefeller his varying political coloration—and how do they work? They have been, in the past and present, an interesting combination of Liberal Republicans and non-active Democrats. These men are amateurs in politics though highly professional in public relations techniques. Alan Otten and Charles Seib, writing in *Harper's,* says of them that "compared to the politically tough Kennedy operators, most of them seem like Rover Boys, still afflicted with the same naïveté which doomed Rockefeller's abortive try for the GOP nomination in late 1959 and 1960." In the current instance, their naïveté will not be important in the in-fighting which will precede the Republican Convention. Experts at winning nominations and losing elections will handle that chore. Then the speech writers and the "strategists" will take over. At that point, the looseleaf notebook which they have prepared for him—and which provides instant policies—would come into play. Though a staff conference with Rockefeller tends to look more like a mass meeting—he now has almost twice as many advisers as Averell Harriman needed to run New York State—the Looseleaf serves the same kind of easy, thinkless function that Plotto used to offer to pulp writers in a less complicated era. "We can put together a definitive speech or statement on practically every important topic within twenty-four hours," an aide told the Otten-Seib collaborators.

No longer among the group of advisers is Emmet John Hughes. Once a *Time* editor, Hughes brought a pretentious prose style and an arrogant disdain for the *polloi* to the

Rockefeller entourage. He is widely credited with having written the speeches and manufactured the verbal hand grenades which Governor Rockefeller tossed at the Republican Party and its leaders in the pre-1960 convention battles. This disregard for the party's good is typical of Hughes—if only because he associated himself with the GOP (first with Eisenhower) in the hope that he could remake it in the image of Liberalism.

The one Republican politician in the group, now that Jud Morhouse has been banished for whatever complicity he may or may not have had in the State Liquor Authority scandals, is George Hinman, a lawyer from the large town of Binghamton. Hinman is Rockefeller's representative on the Republican National Committee and he has been assigned the rough job of winning over delegates to the Rockefeller cause. Also on the inside is William J. Ronan, a political science professor who serves as a technician in state government. He is credited with having given direction to the forty task forces set up by Rockefeller after taking office. These task forces, designed to teach everyone in the state legislature how to legislate, functioned until it threatened a strike if it got any more condescendingly gratuitous advice and unwanted counsel. John Lockwood, a Roosevelt Administration graduate, and Oscar Ruebhausen, who served with Rockefeller on a Truman foreign aid advisory board, are influential members of the "in" group. Where state politics are concerned, Rockefeller leans on his single clearly conservative associate, Lieutenant Governor Malcolm Wilson, who is, however, somewhat suspect to the others. The new hard edge of the Governor's foreign policy utterances can be traced to Henry Kissinger.

Yet, in the final analysis, and as he must, Nelson Rockefeller makes the decisions that count. In recent months, he has paid increasingly less attention to his aides and to those with political savvy who were brought in to the mammoth conferences. This had led to trouble. Despite his years with the Roosevelt, Truman and Eisenhower Administrations in Washington, he has never learned how Congress works. The governor of a large state has a great deal of influence among the members of the delegation in Congress, but he must always make it clear that he is simply offering advice, not giving orders. Rockefeller, however, has on more than one occasion attempted to dictate to the Republican members of the House. The most disastrous case concerned foreign aid. The Kennedy Administration was seeking a foreign aid authorization which would give it a blank check on the Treasury for a period of years. The euphemism for this was "long-term financing." The Congress calls it "back-door spending." The conservative members abhor it because it robs them of their Constitutional right to appropriate on an annual basis and adds to the President's power.

At the request of Secretary of State Dean Rusk, however, Rockefeller bore down on the Republican members from New York State—most of them conservatives. The outcry from the congressmen was loud and indignant. Instead of ducking, as a more experienced man would have done, Rockefeller acted like a political neophyte. In a statement both approving and disapproving the Kennedy maneuver, he said: "While I strongly support long-range planning in foreign aid, I am at the same time opposed to doing it through so-called back-door financing." This tail-in-mouth reaction did much to raise doubts about Rockefeller's perspicacity and focused attention on the fiscal integrity of his administration—of which more later. There have been other snap judgments on episodes, such as when he summoned a special session of the legislature to suspend the New York City school board and to adopt a series of his proposals, only to discover that his plans contained technical errors.

It is on the question of fiscal integrity that Rockefeller has made himself most vulnerable—if only because he took so much credit in that department. In the spring of 1963, the New York legislature cut some $80 million from his budget and an additional $90 million from other levies, a sizable reduction in a state budget. But it also made some vulgar noises at his "look what I did" statement that the cuts had been achieved "with a balanced budget, governmental economy, and pay-as-you-go financing." The nation may not have known, but the men of Albany were aware that New York State's constitution demands a balanced budget. The legislators were even more aware that to balance his budget, Rockefeller had to hold up income tax refunds and payments due to contractors in the final month of the fiscal year.

The New York *World Telegram,* in a page-one story by Frank Lynn, told the sad tale. Rockefeller, said Lynn, boasted of "governmental economy" in his statement:

Some statistics which don't prove his point:

Gov. Averell Harriman's last state budget totaled $1.8 billion. Rockefeller's current budget is $2.8 billion.

The weekly state payroll at the end of Harriman's administration was $9.7 million for 118,000 employes. A recent weekly payroll was $13.7 million for 128,000 state workers.

The budget for Harriman's personal staff was $1.1 million. It is $2 million for Rockefeller. [And this does not count the platoons of aides working for him and paid by him or by Rockefeller enterprises.]

Rockefeller is collecting 85 percent more than Harriman in gasoline, cigarette, inheritance, and state income taxes.

The Rockefeller administration defines pay-as-you-go as a balanced budget without tax-supported bonds.

Democrats charge that Rockefeller's version of pay-as-you-go is a myth, costs the taxpayers more, and borders on the unconstitutional.

Two examples of this myth are cited. Though the voters authorized a bond issue to build mental hospitals, Rockefeller refuses to follow this method because it would violate his pay-as-you-go principles. Instead, he proposes to have the State Housing Finance Agency issue its own bonds, build the hospitals, and lease them to the state for fifty years at a rental equal to interest and amortization. But the Housing Agency must pay interest of about one percent more than the state. "Translating this into dollars and cents," the *World Telegram* noted, "$100 million in bonds floated under the Rockefeller plan will cost $90 million more in interest over fifty years than the fifteen-year state bond issue." The second example of pay-as-you-go is his plan for constructing state government buildings not authorized by the legislature. The cities will construct these buildings and rent them to the state. Since the cities pay a higher interest rate, the cost will be higher than if Rockefeller had gotten authorization and then issued bonds.

Put together, the pieces of the Rockefeller jigsaw explained why his stock had begun to slip badly by June 1963. As one reporter told Otten and Seib, "He always had the arrogance of wealth, but back in 1958 and '59 he at least realized he had a lot to learn about government and politics. Now he thinks he knows as much as Roosevelt, Truman, and Kennedy together." This was hardly a fair statement. It was not arrogance, any more than the stubbornness of an adolescent is arrogance. Like other political figures before him, he was forced to learn in the glare of public attention. He could boast that he was a "practical do-gooder" but it requires more than that to run an enterprise as vast as New York State. The temptation is always to impose the executive will—as if New York were Standard Oil, the Chase Bank, or any one of the incredibly diverse Rockefeller enterprises. And since his philosophy of government was, to use his own word, "activist," he was doing what came naturally. Rockefeller believes in big government and in a President who can "control" that government—the White House, the vast Executive Branch and its bureaucracy, the Congress.

It is possible that by the use of astute public relations, Rockefeller might have restored his dwindling prestige and relustered his image. Though time was running out and those passionately committed to a Barry Goldwater Presidential nomination had other plans, much might have been done to arrest the toboggan in its course. But Rockefeller had lost his best public relations adviser, Francis Jamieson. Jamieson's death opened the way for Emmet John Hughes. Since then there has been nobody to help him who really knows politics, newspapermen, or the public. But the best of counsel could not have done anything for Nelson Rockefeller after June 1963, when he remarried. His divorce from Mary Todhunter Rockefeller had hurt him in his 1962 reelection contest—or so insisted the pundits, who would not accept the other indices of weakness.

The marriage to "Happy" Murphy came as a shock, and brought in its wake a collection of ugly rumors. These stories aside, the face-up facts startled his supporters around the country. After 31 years, he had divorced one wife, the mother of his five children, then waited until "Happy" Murphy got her divorce to marry her. Most damaging was the clear impression which neither Rockefeller nor his new wife refuted that she had given up legal custody of her four children by her first marriage. There had been rumors of the impending marriage, but no one had predicted the violence of the impact. Women, particularly those who had been married for many years, felt a personal sense of betrayal.

Mrs. Phyllis Schlafly, president of the Illinois Federation of Republican Women, said angrily: "I've been taking a poll of Republican women I meet all over the state, and their reaction is nearly unanimous—they're disgusted with Rockefeller. A man who has broken up two homes is not the kind we want for high public office. The party is not so hard up that it can't find somebody who stuck by his own family."

The feeling among the professionals nevertheless remained one of wait-and-see. Many felt that much of the outrage was due to a belief among those who expressed it that Rockefeller was flaunting his power, wealth, and position by acting so flagrantly against the prevailing *mores*. But consternation struck the Rockefeller forces when one of his friends and supporters, former Republican Senator Prescott Bush of Connecticut, made headlines with a commencement address at an upper-class girls' school. His speech, described by *Time* as "one of the most wrathful public lashings in memory," cut to the quick:

"Have we come to the point where one of the great political parties will confer upon such a one its highest and greatest responsibility? I venture to hope not. . . . Have our standards shifted so much? I venture to hope not."

To make matters worse—and to reinforce those who felt that the marriage was an affront—Rockefeller and his bride made news by attending a charity fair aboard a ship that withdrew past the three-mile limit for an evening of gambling and dancing. Among the guests were the Duke and Duchess of Windsor—and the photographer caught the four greeting each other. This graphic juxtaposition of the man who gave up his throne for "the woman I love" and another man who might have surrendered his chance at a Presidential nomination did not escape the public.

Would Rockefeller be able to ride out the storm? He obviously believed so. But the surge of Goldwater strength suddenly became a boom. In states which were considered Rockefeller territory, as far as delegates to the 1964 convention, the news was all bad. By July of 1963, the politicians were certain that Nelson Rockefeller could get the convention votes of New York State and nothing else. From Republican state chairman down to the rank and file, the reaction was almost unanimously a thumbs-down on Rockefeller. There were, of course, some exceptions. Thomas E. Dewey announced that Nelson Rockefeller was still "the logical nominee."

Dewey's logic was not, however, the logic of most Republicans. If in convention assembled they chased after the pied pipers of Eastern Liberal Republicans it was not for reasons of political logic. It was, moreover, difficult for them to forget Rockefeller's attack during the Eisenhower years on those Republicans they respected. Then, in a battle over foreign aid within the Administration, Rockefeller had said curiously to the Washington *Post*'s Chalmers Roberts that there were two factions in the Republican Party. One faction was "represented by [Treasury Secretary George] Humphrey and 'his men' throughout the government. This faction would have the United States act abroad only on an anti-Communist basis in order to deny this or that nation to the enemy. These people are the new style isolationists." The others, of which he was one, believed that "foreign aid must be an obligation of the freest people on earth."

They would remember a Washington column by William S. White in which he noted: "Governor Rockefeller is evolving a political posture not unlike that of President Harry Truman. Mr. Truman was usually prepared to give the liberals almost anything in the way of welfare legislation." But most of all, the conservatives of South, West, and Northwest would remember that even a ballplayer is only allowed three strikes. There had been one Willkie and two Deweys. The Eastern Liberals had boasted that they could win, whereas the conservative Robert Taft could not. They had told the voters that Liberalism's program was good—but that they could carry it out better.

Republicans had moved ahead. They had seen the New Frontier bring economic stagnation and an unemployment rate which remained at a tragically high level. They had seen American prestige skid to an all-time low and Communist insolence tolerated and unchecked. But most of all, they knew that the Eastern wing of the Republican Party was an albatross and a voodoo. It could win nominations, but when the election rolled around, it was elsewhere detained. Governor Nelson Rockefeller, for all his charm and his good intentions, for all his humanity and his ambition, was a loser. The mathematics said he was. The polls said he was. And the most elementary common sense knew he was.

For a while, even George Gallup admitted it.

X

GEORGE ROMNEY AND
THE NEIGHING OF DARK HORSES

Obviously, Nelson Rockefeller believed that the bad public reaction to his remarriage would wear off. The kingmakers were not so sure. When the Presbyterian Church board formally censured the minister who had performed the marriage ceremony, and other denominations echoed the view of an Episcopal weekly which stated a strong doubt that Rockefeller could "any longer be considered as a candidate for the Presidency," the case against his candidacy became stronger. One thing was clear in the first response: Republican politicians who had gone along with Rockefeller though preferring Barry Goldwater had seized on the remarriage to justify a switch. Perhaps that quiet telephone call from one or another representative of the Rockefeller business empire would bring about still another change of heart. But it seemed more than likely, as the pre-campaign for the nomination progressed, that the sides might be chosen before the memory of Rockefeller's remarriage had dimmed sufficiently to permit a comeback.

Too many Republican leaders were busily committing themselves to Goldwater or to favorite sons. Once the promise has been made it can of course be broken, but there are penalties involved. And as one anti-Goldwater, anti-Rockefeller, anti-politician observer said of an important Eastern Republican leader, "How many sinking ships can he desert in one year?" The death—or at least the critical illness—of the Rockefeller candidacy could be gauged by a number of signs. On the psychological level, former adherents were saying with an all-for-love look in their eyes that Governor Rockefeller had remarried fully cognizant of the effect on his political fortunes because happiness was more important. On the psychological warfare side, political publicists close to General Eisenhower no longer felt it necessary to hide what insiders had long known—namely, that the former President did not like Rockefeller. (Eisenhower was irritated at what he considered Rockefeller's "pushiness" during his Washington period.) On the strategic side, the Rockefeller forces hastily set out to form a coalition of favorite sons who could prevent Barry Goldwater from sewing up state delegations. (This has never worked, but it is always tried by the desperate.)

Of prime significance was clear-cut and incontrovertible evidence that the Eastern Liberal wing was shopping for a new candidate. There were possibilities in plenty—governors, senators, congressmen, and would-be Willkies by the score. The problem was to get one of sufficient stature to replace Nelson Rockefeller, and one who could use the "Goldwater can't win but I can" line without causing guffaws among the gentlemen of the press. He would also have to be sufficiently well known to be an instant candidate, or at least one who did not require too many months of Madison Avenue treatment. A weak candidate would encourage a Rockefeller counterstroke, thereby dividing Republican Liberals and strengthening Goldwater.

There were parlous few possibilities who measured up—in fact, none. The Rockefeller name is part of the nation's folklore. It has worked itself into the language and the poetry of Tin Pan Alley. Governor Rockefeller, moreover, has been the beneficiary of widespread speculation in the mass media ever since he defeated Governor Averell Harriman in what was then ironically called the Battle of the Titans. That was in 1958—and by mid-1963 the amount of newsprint and air time devoted to Rockefeller's chances at the Republican Presidential nomination could easily have put over a new candy bar. Since the 1962 elections, however, several names have been injected into the discussions of 1964. One was Governor William Scranton who had returned Pennsylvania to the Republican column by a handy half million votes. True, his name meant little more to most Americans than a coal town. Few were certain where he stood, perhaps because he never allowed an alleged pro-Liberalism to become anticonservatism. But Governor Scranton seemed genuinely lacking in the proper desire for the nomination. He practiced the ritual coyness of public figures in his position, but his disclaimers had a ring of sincerity. If he did not want the nomination, no one would twist his arm to force him to accept it. Even General Eisenhower, in 1951, never went beyond saying, "Don't shove me so fast." Scranton would accept a favorite son draft, perhaps with an eye to the Vice-Presidency. (According to Pennsylvania law, a governor is allowed only one term and the next Senate seat to come up is held by Republican Hugh Scott.)

Another reluctant candidate was Senator Thruston B. Morton. It is said that he has no desire whatsoever for the nomination. To this, he has added a fast amen, adding: "In terms of political reality, I have no intention of seeking a place on the national ticket. I have a comfortable six-year term ahead in the Senate, and the Senate is the height of my ambition. I'm not even coming out of the starting gate on this one."

Events may rule otherwise. Morton—a friendly and persuasive man with the kind of looks and manner which attract women without offending men—has proved to be an impressive vote getter. After three terms in the House of Representatives, he won election to the Senate from his state of Kentucky. In 1962 he upset the poll takers and the pundits by easily swamping a popular Democrat amply supported by Americans for Democratic Action, the labor bosses, and the Administration. A number of conservative Republican leaders had been looking over Thruston Morton fairly carefully when it seemed possible that Goldwater would refuse categorically to run. Morton once remarked that he was "two degrees to the left of center," but that was some time ago. He has with increasing frequency associated himself with the conservative side—and he is said to favor Goldwater. Of all the Republican possibilities other than Goldwater, Morton is the only one who would have any degree of acceptance in the South. Being from Kentucky, he would meet little of the resistance that goes to most Northerners. The conservatives talked of Morton as a substitute for what they really wanted because, as Chairman of the Republican National Committee, he had given them a fair shake. They felt that his period of service with the committee and his present post as successor to Goldwater in the chairmanship of the Republican Senate Campaign Committee had projected him before the party leaders on many levels. And General Eisenhower has listed him among those he thought would make a good President, an endorsement which would probably have weight with the 1964 delegates.

The man most often mentioned as the sucessor to Nelson Rockefeller in the affections of the Eastern Liberal wing, however, is Governor George Romney of Michigan. Romney, a devout Mormon holding a rank comparable to bishop in the Church of Jesus Christ of Latter-day Saints, said he fasted before coming to a decision on running for Michigan's governorship. It is now being suggested by those who do not like him that his intention to seek the Presidency became obvious when he began serving drinks to his guests. Mormons do not drink, smoke, gamble, or swear, and Romney's parties had been as dry as sand. This has now changed, though Romney and his family remain innocent and sober bystanders to the drinking. (The change took place, of course, when Romney realized that his teetotalism was leading guests to arrive primed for a night under his personal Volstead Act.)

A more likely indicator was Romney's sudden appearance, late in June of 1963, uninvited, at the head of a group of NAACP antisegregation marchers in the fashionable Grosse Pointe suburb of Detroit. Romney is an informal man, and this act may have been his unconventional way of showing solidarity with the civil rights agitation. But the timing made it suspect. It had, moreover, the unmistakable *cachet* of the Madison Avenue image makers.

It was regrettable, too, because it was not necessary. From the moment that Rockefeller seemed rocky, however, Romney had gotten the nod from the kingmakers. Like every putative Republican nominee since 1940, he had been given the Willkie buildup. Stories filled the media on this successful executive who walks among the people, the slightly but not

too eccentric politico, the man above party. The plan, however, had been to build him up gradually so as to give the
boom a semblance of spontaneity. The realization that the
Rockefeller crisis was a grave one, that popularity was not
just around the corner for him, prompted the sudden push
to make Romney known. Two trips to Washington, one of
them including an appearance before the National Press
Club—guarantee of nationwide attention—were used to give
him star billing. He paid his tribute to the big-city states by
attacking those "too many" (unspecified) who demand States'
rights because they "want to make the states into a road block
to progress." Criticizing those who wish to bring the Constitution and the courts back into focus, he argued that
"mutilation of the Federal government is not the answer
to growing problems of centralization." And he demonstrated
why he was so glowingly eulogized by the moderately Liberal
weekly, *The Reporter*. Except for his urging that labor submit to antitrust legislation, there was little in his program to
annoy the "Vital Center."

It cannot be gainsaid that to those Americans aware of his
existence, Romney would have some appeal. His business
record, running the 1954–1957 American Motors deficit of
$28.5 million into a 1958–1961 profit of $158.2 million, was
recommendation enough of business acumen. That he res-
cued millions of Americans from the tyranny of overstuffed
cars and tailfins should have earned him their gratitude. But
beyond that, where did he stand as a political figure? Was it
enough to say that he had undoubted and admirable virtues—
a good and happy home life, devotion to his church, honor
and integrity—or that the highest of motives were sufficient
background and preparation for the Presidency? Would his
quick grasp of the gimmick—his Citizens' Thursday in which

any Michigander can have five minutes by the timer of his attention—make him the more fitted to live up to the responsibilities of the world's hardest job? These were questions to be answered.

Of all the doubts expressed about George Romney, only one could be answered flatly in his favor: Can a person born outside the borders of the United States (Romney was born in Mexico of parents who had emigrated to avoid the anti-polygamy laws of this country) serve as President? The Constitution seemed to steep the answer in ambiguity by stating that "no person except a natural born citizen . . . shall be eligible for the office of President." Though the courts had never ruled on this, the First Congress had in 1790 clarified the Constitution by defining "natural born" in the Uniform Rule of Naturalization Act: "The children of citizens of the United States that may be born beyond sea, or outside the limits of the United States, shall be considered as natural born citizens of the United States." On this there could be no debate.

But, if it mattered at all to the kingmakers, was Romney a Republican? His first job, in 1928, was as a tariff specialist on the staff of the Democratic Senator David I. Walsh of Massachusetts. This would be of no signficance had he not made such a point of his opposition to all political parties and his rather childish reluctance in 1962 when he ran for governor to be identified with the party which nominated him. Or, prior to that, his statement that he was "forced" to announce Republican affiliation when he ran for the post of delegate to the convention which rewrote the Michigan constitution. Having based his campaign to win ratification for the new constitution, and his successful gubernatorial race on the nonpartisan Citizens for Michigan, he began calling for a

Citizens of America which would have neither ties nor association with any political organization. William H. Hessler
pointed out in *The Reporter* that Romney

wants to foster political action by citizens in their capacity as individuals, not as members of groups or blocs—not in unions or
corporations or even in political parties. It might not be too much
to say he likes to visualize the correct political process for America
as one gigantic town meeting, instead of an aggregation of blocs
and interest groups. Early in the [constitutional] convention session, Romney made some speeches around the state in which he
seemed cold to party politics. He was looking for something he
called a consensus of citizens.

Though such an idea would appeal to the academic community which is never at ease among politicians, it would
drive the professionals wild—and not solely because their jobs
may be at stake. They know that the two-party system was not
planned by devious men. It grew out of the needs implicit in
the Constitution. It serves a vital purpose in channelizing the
political will. Without political parties there would be
anarchy. The suggestion that they be scrapped has come up
frequently and as frequently has been forgotten simply because it would mean the end of representative government.
Without parties, the popular will could be made manifest
only through riots and demonstrations—or through revolution. Of importance in winning the support of the professionals was some assurance that they would not be ousted
or ignored, which Citizens for America seemed to indicate.
Romney was told firmly to cease and desist.

In other matters, Romney has shown a kind of unformu-
lated thought which can hardly appeal to the average Republican or win him the kind of organizational support without

which he will not even be able to see Kennedy's dust in any electoral race. For example, he has repeatedly warned that it is "wrong" for businessmen to organize politically. His reason has a dubious ring: "We need greater citizen participation in meeting our political and economic problems," he says—adding that it is not right for people "to exercise their citizenship on the basis of their economic interest or affiliation." This must mean something to Romney, but all it seems to say is that businessmen aren't citizens.

This vagueness is apparent in his "policies" on labor-management relations. Labor, he says, has grown too big for proper collective bargaining. Business is too big. Government should stay out. Nevertheless, he urges that the labor-management conflict "must be resolved before we can again resume the type of economic progress of which we are capable." . . . "The nation," he says, "cannot exist half free and half monopolistic." Therefore compel business to remain within certain arbitrary limits of size. No company should be allowed to control more than 35 percent of its industry. Not their business practices or the possibility that they may be monopolistic are the criteria. Bigness is enough to make Romney say, "Off with their excess-over-35-percent"—particularly in the automotive industry where American Motors has nowhere near that percentage of the market. To quote Hessler in *The Reporter*: "If Romney has spelled out anywhere precisely what he would do with big labor, I haven't found it; nor could I get it from him in person."

Romney tends to lose his sense of judgment when goaded, and to speak in simplistic and self-defeating terms of complex matters. Faced by the problem of the John Birch Society, Romney ducked it completely and then tried to change the subject angrily by raising the issue of Communist infiltration of the government and the Democratic Party. He was not, however, prepared with documentation, nor had he the political sophistication to handle it properly. It was just a blast about a touchy matter. The basic understanding was lacking, so that what he said tended to sound like wild talk. Turning on his bedevilers, Romney charged that the Democratic Party's extremist group

is the Communist Party elements. Their problem is in the form of Communism, not in the form of Birchism. That has been historically true. In the last thirty to thirty-five years, the Communists have worked themselves into positions of importance not only in government but in the ranks of the [Democratic] party. I think that Communism is still a problem within the Democratic Party.

What Romney meant to say was one thing. What he actually said was that the Democratic Party was thoroughly infiltrated —a statement of deadly import in Walter Reuther's Michigan. Caught in the cross fire of Democratic indignation, Romney made matters worse by "explaining" what he meant. Denying that he had said "there were Communists in the Democratic Party at the present time," he added that it would not "knowingly harbor" Communists and that both parties "must be constantly on the alert" to prevent infiltration. The remark, however, remains on the record—and it will live to plague Romney whenever he runs for elective office again.

As a would-be Presidential candidate, Romney is already being called on the vagueness of his foreign policy thinking. So far it consists of pious platitudes of such vast generality that they are meaningless. Stewart Alsop, whose *Saturday Evening Post* assignments take him everywhere, seemed much impressed by the Romney messianism. But his summation of the Romney foreign policy stance leaves much to be desired, as Alsop himself realized:

> Romney's foreign policy thinking goes back in its essentials to . . . the Mormon thesis that the divinely inspired American system will lead to the adoption of "the American concept," and the "worldwide application of our principles" will in the end "remove peoples everywhere from bondage. . . ."

The details remain to be filled in—it is hard, for example, to see just how "our principles" are to be applied to such complex situations as those in Berlin or Southeast Asia.

Or, Constant Reader would venture, to the cannibal lands of Africa, the oligarchies of the Middle East, or the dictatorships of Latin America. Romney, however, sees the world in evangelical terms. His talk of "removing peoples everywhere from bondage" will, moreover, smack of hypocrisy to voters who recall that the Mormon Church considers all Negroes the "sons of Ham" and a race with a curse on it. Though Romney has always opposed discrimination, the Democrats will not let him forget that he remains a leader among Mormons. The reminders may not be made on coast-to-coast television, but they will be heard.

The Romney that emerges after even the most superficial study recalls William Jennings Bryan—in a Brooks Brothers suit. His utterances all have the simplistic fervor of the "cross of gold" speech, and like Bryan he is all ambition. "When he sees the brass ring coming round," Alsop quotes an associate, "he can't help grabbing for it." But fervor and missionary zeal have in the past failed to do the trick. They failed for Bryan three times. They failed repeatedly for Henry A. Wallace, whom Romney resembles in many ways. As a Presidential candidate he would be, despite his business training, out in the wild blue yonder. He would be preaching a utopian gospel of politics, deeply sincere and thoroughly unrelated to everyday matters.

The times call for more than that. A Presidential candidate must be a product of the political machine or have a movement of his own. He must be a John F. Kennedy who knows the old ways to power or a Barry Goldwater who blazes his own trail. Romney would appeal to millions of Americans, as did Wendell Willkie. They would look at him fondly—and vote for the other fellow.

XI

GOLDWATER—MAN AND SYMBOL

In the spring of 1963, House Republican Whip Leslie Arends of Illinois said, "A year ago, a vast majority of Republicans—myself included—believed that Kennedy would be unbeatable. Now we think he's vulnerable and that we have a good chance to knock him off next year." These sentiments were echoed across the land by enthusiastic Republicans. They smelled victory because, on the one hand, the Kennedy Administration sank daily more deeply into a morass of its own making and, on the other hand, because they had a candidate.

For the first time in decades, Republican leaders at every level were spurred by the kind of grass-roots enthusiasm they had almost forgotten. The cause of the enthusiasm was Barry Morris Goldwater, Senator from Arizona, Mr. Conservative, and reinvigorator of the Republican Party.

Since that time, GOP politicians have spent days and hours at the arithmetic of proving that a conservative can beat President Kennedy in 1964. They needn't have bothered. Barry Goldwater was their proof. Coming up from behind, he had pulled strongly ahead of Governor Nelson Rockefeller. Only a miracle could dissipate that lead and project Rockefeller into the candidacy. That lead was all that Goldwater needed to silence the doubting Thomases and to unleash his vociferously eager supporters. The spotlight had turned toward him because of his unabashed conservatism and the response it evoked in young voters and old. But Goldwater himself had kept it focused on him. He is a man who has that undefinable quality the intellectuals call charisma. Long ago, the perceptive professionals had noticed that quality in Goldwater. When he spoke, the audiences seemed almost electronically to duplicate the expression on his face—the smile, the frown, the seriousness. In this time of Madison Avenue "image," he draws the voters to him because they can sense that he is a completely engaged man. Win, lose or draw, he is ready to fight for his political philosophy to the bitter end.

This was something the Republican Party had long sought. In 1960, Richard Nixon had offered another form of engagement—his long love affair with politics. But Goldwater has had an uninterrupted love affair—with people. And the people have responded.

The validity of this was no more apparent than during and after the great July 4, 1963, "Draft Goldwater" rally in Washington's National Armory. Only the picketing members of the American Nazi Party hated Goldwater. The Liberal newspapermen covering the rally could not really succumb to their ideological antagonism. They disagree violently with Goldwater but they both like and respect him. They cannot resort to the kind of slingshot attack they used to cut Richard Nixon down. The low blow and the loaded sentence comes hard to them when they write about Goldwater. After the Rockefeller remarriage, moreover, when the Goldwater path to the Republican Presidential nomination seemed like a royal road, they were constrained by his possible political ascendancy. But they were also responding to the remarkable Goldwater personality—remarkable precisely because it is not, in the Madison Avenue sense, a "personality" at all. He is a man you like and respect.

And that, more than all the arithmetical proof, is why Barry Goldwater and Goldwater conservatism feel they are on the winning side.

That too is why the Kennedy Administration will move heaven and earth to deprive him of the Republican nomination for the Presidency. John F. Kennedy looked warmly human against the completely cerebral Richard Nixon in the 1960 campaign. Against Goldwater, he will appear like a piece of well-designed ice sculpture. The conservatives will be voting for Goldwater because he is Mr. Conservative and because he has carried the ball for their political and philosophical beliefs since the death of Robert A. Taft. The so-called "average American" will cast a Goldwater vote for the same reason that millions voted for Harry S. Truman. "Don't ask me about party platforms," one voter told this writer in 1948. "I'm voting for Harry Truman because I think he's on my side." In spite of the poison gas attack on conservatism which has filled the press and the airwaves these many years, Goldwater can still evoke this kind of response. The Democrats, in 1960, turned voters against Nixon by asking, "Would you buy a used car from him?" They won't employ this tactic against Goldwater.

What then will be the strategy of Democrats to defeat Goldwater, and of Liberal Republicans to prevent him from getting the nomination? In the weeks and months to come, new forms of attack will be devised, striking not directly at him but at his ideas, his political philosophy, and at those who are working night and day in his behalf. That these will be inaccurate or unfair is irrelevant. Gentle Reader, that is politics. But since those attacks will come—have, in fact, already come—it is important to understand the methodology. If the methodology is clear, then any new line will be patently obvious and ineffectual.

Anti-conservatives—and those who would use the South as a whipping boy—have been arguing that the Goldwater reliance on winning over that once-solidly Democratic preserve will turn the GOP into a "white man's party."

The implication in this warning to the GOP to stay out of the South is clearly that to venture in will "prove" that Goldwater and his supporters are racists. Again logic would demand that Democratic reliance on Southern votes (and on the support of anti-Negro trade unions) would make President Kennedy an exponent of Jim Crow—but why belabor this point? The pundits never bother to make these distinctions and parallels. But it might be interesting to compare Barry Goldwater's record on the treatment of Negroes with that of the President, his multitudinous family, or any leading Democrat. The result would be laughable. And when the differences in approach are discussed, it would be shown that Senator Goldwater has a genuine dislike for any system which forgets that the brotherhood of man is related to the Fatherhood of God. Goldwater, however, also believes that Heaven is not stormed by the bayonets of Federal troops. In his own experience and through his own efforts, he achieved a great deal more by persuasion in his home city than the Democrats have accomplished by force. To Barry Goldwater, force is not the answer. Force has never succeeded in convincing a man that he is wrong; it can only show him that it is better to submit than to go to jail. But in submitting to force, he becomes the prisoner of his emotions. If he is persuaded, he is henceforth a missionary.

Barry Goldwater appeals to the South for reasons highly remote from the segregation issue. But it would be foolish to deny that this issue does not enter into the thinking of many people north and south of the Mason and Dixon Line who see their homes and property threatened by Federal coercion. They are not segregationists or integrationists; they are people with a problem. They do not want a pistol pointed at them. They want to work out the problem peacefully and equitably, both to themselves and to the minorities. Therefore, the Goldwater background is meaningful to them—or would be, if the pundits were not working overtime to obscure it. What, then, is his record? Here are the facts:

In 1946–47, Goldwater took a voluntary reduction in his Air Force rank in order to organize the Arizona Air National Guard. As its executive officer, he established an integrated National Guard—the first to take this step. As a member of the Phoenix City Council, he took the initiative (at the request of the Negro community) to desegregate the restaurant at the municipal airport. This was the first quality restaurant in Phoenix to admit Negro customers. During this period, he also led the movement to desegregate movie theatres. He contributed substantially to the Urban League.

The employment policy of the Goldwater department stores has always been integrated. Negroes, Mexicans, and Indians attend employee meetings, enjoy the same benefits, and use all facilities in the stores. The Goldwater attitude does not only embrace Negroes. On the Navaho Indian reservation, he is known as "Mr. America" because of his many errands of mercy—transporting Indians to hospitals on emergency calls and helping to look after the people. Many older Indians, whose English is at best primitive, call airplanes "goldwaters" because of his shuttle flights in their aid. To the chagrin of his opponents, Arizona Indians have been registering Republican at the rate of seven-to-one. None of this has become general knowledge because Goldwater has not hired publicity men to tell the tale. Nor has he stood on the floor of the Senate, tears running down his cheeks, to describe his great humanitarian soul. There are actions which men of good will take but do not advertise. And because Goldwater believes that the conflict of the races can only be solved by a change in the national feeling—both black and white—he has nothing more dramatic to offer but the truth.

The civil rights issue, however, is a foundling on the Democratic doorstep. The leaders of Negro organizations know that the Kennedy Administration has the votes and the power to ram through any measure it pleases. The power of sit-ins and mass demonstrations will be aimed from now until Election Day 1964 at the New Frontier. Barry Goldwater will triumph at the Republican convention in San Francisco on the basis of a good many other factors—ideological, psychological, personal, and political. His biggest asset is that he represents a new mood in American politics. He is the symbol of conservatism on the march—the conservatism of young intellectuals who have (to set the Lincoln Steffans quotation on its ear) seen the Democratic future and know it doesn't work. They are voters who lived through the trauma of the 1950s as students and now wonder why the execution of Joe McCarthy didn't bring enlightenment and jolly-o to the United States. They do not see materializing the brave new world of Kennedyism. The tailfins have been removed from the automobiles—but this did not bring a new dedication to freedom or a return to prosperity. The rate of economic growth has

slowed down from what it was under the moderate conservatism of the Eisenhower era—and unemployment, which was
to vanish once the Kennedy Klub took over, remains stubbornly unbudgeable. The young intellectuals—and their influence is far greater than their numbers, as we learned when
they faced Left during the Roosevelt era—are bored with the
conformity of the present Establishment. They are in revolt
against bad economic thinking, bad aesthetics, and bad moral-
ity. They know that the United States has traded its national
purpose for a mess of slogans. The anti-Communism which
was presumably ingrained in the American people has
withered away within the Federal bureaucracy.

Barry Goldwater is the answer to the vast wasteland of
American Liberalism. He speaks out in terms that are intellectually respectable but not intellectually forbidding. And,
mirabile dictu, he is not afraid to call a New Frontier spade a
damned shovel. The young intellectuals who pack the Goldwater rallies or who stand on chairs in college auditoriums to
hear him speak have taken to Barry Goldwater after their first
visceral response to him by studying his position on the
issues. The politicians within the Republican Party who are
ready to lay it on the line for him have studied the response
of the young intellectuals, the married couples with new
mortgages, the idealists who have read Keynes and Marx and
John Galbraith, but find Hayek and von Mises more lucid.
The great middle class which made this country and sustains
it today cries for Barry Goldwater because he thinks in concrete terms of their problems.

Excerpts from Goldwater speeches put in capsule form his
position on the issues. As a Portable Goldwater, they do the
job:

On Politics:

Up to the first of the year, I frankly felt that it would be next to impossible to beat him [President Kennedy] in 1964, but it has been a combination, a compiling of errors that has changed my view. Cuba is part of it. The situation with France is another part. Skybolt in England and the Polaris. Canada. The domestic economy not moving forward rapidly enough. Unemployment that plagues us. Instead of reducing expenditures so we can reduce taxes, he is asking more and more expenditures. Issues are piling up to the point that, unless some miracle happens in the next 16 or 18 months, I think he can be beaten.

* * *

I charge that there is today a cynical alliance between the politicians who call themselves liberal and the corrupt big-city machines whose job it is to deliver the bloc votes of the big Northern cities. It is the corrupt big-city machines which elect these men to public office. I charge that the politicians who have inherited the tradition of liberalism in this country today are not liberals at all, but merely ambitious men who have become the captives of the big-city machines.

* * *

I think that the Republican Party has only one position, and that is a position to the "right." ... I do not mean by that, that the Republican Party go to the "far right," nor that it become a middle-of-the-road party. There are millions and millions of conservatives in this country in both parties who are concerned lest conservatism be stamped out. ... The only place the Republican Party can occupy is a position to the right of center.

On Government Spending:

We cannot afford to leave the destiny of our great nation in the hands of men who actually believe that spending money is the basic solution to all problems.

* * *

The naïve and narrow idea that spending our resources in larger quantities will somehow solve every dangerous and complex problem of foreign and domestic policy is the characteristic —and fatal—weakness of the liberals. They are obsessed with the economic solutions for every problem.

* * *

Public debt mounts to astronomical heights and cannot be paid off except by ruinous inflation or repudiation. The federal debt is a time bomb hanging over the security of our people. . . . Have you ever seen such outrageous taxation, such a staggering national debt, such waste of public money, such a pyramid of Government subsidies, dangerous inflation, so many lavish political promises, such a gigantic federal bureaucracy, so much Government favoritism to special groups, such moral laxity and so little responsibility in public life?

* * *

This 100-billion-dollar spending plan [the budget for fiscal year 1964], combined with tax reduction and a planned deficit of 12 billion dollars, is nothing but a calculated program of inflation. It will weaken the dollar, boost prices and increase the pressure from labor unions for new and exorbitant wage-and-hour demands.

On Foreign Aid:

What could be more foolish than the belief that our good friends will become enemies if we stop paying them?

* * *

We should adopt a discriminating foreign-aid policy. Aid should be furnished only to friendly, anti-Communist nations that are willing to join with us in the struggle for freedom. Moreover, our aid should take the form of loans or technical assistance, not gifts. And we should insist that such nations contribute their fair share to the common cause.

* * *

Increasingly, our foreign aid goes not to our friends, but to professed neutrals—and even to professed enemies. We furnish this aid under the theory that we can buy the allegiance of foreign peoples—or at least discourage them from "going Communist"—by making them economically prosperous. This has been called the "stomach theory of Communism" and it implies that a man's politics are determined by the amount of food in his belly. Everything we have learned from experience and from our observation of the nature of man refutes this theory.

* * *

I feel that proper doctrine to guide foreign aid would have to be based upon the goals of our own national security. It would not be a doctrine of vague altruism but of concrete effort to extend freedom. It would recognize the vastly different capacities of vastly different nations to absorb aid and use it advantageously in terms of building free institutions. It would certainly never approach the struggle between East and West as a mere exercise in bribery, with the booty going to the side that promises to spend more.

* * *

Our present policy of government-to-government aid strengthens socialism in those countries. We are not only perpetuating the inefficiency and waste that always attends government-controlled economies; by strengthening the hand of those governments, we are making it more difficult for free enterprise to take hold. For this reason alone, we should eliminate all government-to-government capital assistance and encourage substitution of American private investment.

On Labor:

Graft and corruption are symptoms of the illness that besets the labor movement, not the cause of it. The cause is the enormous economic and political power now concentrated in the hands of union leaders.

*   *   *

I strongly favor enactment of State "right to work" laws which forbid contracts that make union membership a condition of employment. These laws are aimed at removing a great blight on the contemporary American scene, and I am at a loss to understand why so many people who so often profess concern for civil rights and civil liberties are vehemently opposed to them.

*   *   *

One way to check the unions' power is for the Government to dictate through compulsory arbitration the terms of employment throughout an entire industry. I am opposed to this course because it simply transfers economic power from the unions to the Government, and encourages state socialism.

*   *   *

Let us henceforth make war on all monopolies—whether corporate or union. The enemy of freedom is unrestrained power, and the champions of freedom will fight against the concentration of power wherever they find it.

*   *   *

Unions exist, presumably, to confer economic advantages on their members, not to perform political services for them. Unions should therefore be forbidden to engage in any kind of political activity. . . . I see no reason for labor unions—or corporations—to participate in politics.

*   *   *

We must never destroy the workers' right to strike. We must control it where it applies to the national defense and the operation of the Federal Government.

*   *   *

My bill . . . contains a strike-vote procedure based on the following simple requirements:

First, a strike shall be unlawful unless notice of intention to strike is given to all those concerned at least 30 days prior to the actual beginning of the strike; and,

Second, at any time after such notice has been given, a petition may be filed with the National Labor Relations Board by an employe in the enterprise to be affected, asking the Board to conduct an election by secret ballot among the employes in the establishment to be or being struck, on the question of whether they favor a strike or its continuation. If such a petition is supported by 30 per cent of said employes, the Board shall conduct such an election and the strike or its continuation shall be lawful only if a majority, so voting, cast their ballots in favor thereof.

On Taxes:

The idea that a man who makes $100,000 a year should be forced to contribute 90 per cent of his income to the cost of government, while the man who makes $10,000 is made to pay 20 per cent is repugnant to my notions of justice. I do not believe in punishing success.

*   *   *

The graduated tax is a confiscatory tax.

*   *   *

I believe that, as a practical matter, spending cuts must come before tax cuts. If we reduce taxes before firm-principled decisions are made about expenditures, we will court deficit spending and the inflationary effects that invariably follow.

I wouldn't want to see a tax reduction without first a reduction in the domestic budget. But I'll say this, that we have to have a tax reduction in this country within the next year or two, or I feel we're going to have economic trouble. Now I say that small business cannot expand due to one thing, and that's the tax picture. . . . And, in business, you either expand or you die.

* * *

We should have the kind of liberalization of our tax laws that would permit quick write-off depreciation and put an immediate spur to the economy by enabling our industrial plants to begin large-scale replacement of some 95 billion dollars in obsolete equipment with which they presently are saddled. President Kennedy's gesture of a tax credit in this direction was laughable, and the businessmen who said they wanted it were not for any long-range improvement in the economy.

On Civil Rights:

I continue to believe that it is both wise and just for Negro children to attend the same schools as whites. But I believe the matter of school integration is left to the States under the Tenth Amendment.

* * *

When I consider the over-all issue of civil rights, I come back to the concept that the States have all the rights not specifically reserved to the Federal Government in the Constitution.

* * *

As a merchant, I feel that a man in business who advertises for customers to come to his store . . . and to make purchases from him cannot deny that customer, regardless of race, creed or color, the opportunity to purchase in any department of that store or business.

* * *

I have great respect for the Supreme Court as an institution, but I cannot believe that I display that respect by submitting abjectly to abuses of power by the Court and by condoning its unconstitutional trespass into the legislative sphere of government.

* * *

Despite the recent holding of the Supreme Court, I am firmly convinced not only that integrated schools are not required but that the Constitution does not permit any interference whatsoever by the Federal Government in the field of education.

It may be just or wise or expedient for Negro children to attend the same schools as white children, but they do not have a civil right to do so which is protected by the Federal Constitution or which is enforceable by the Federal Government.

On Big Government:

We don't need the Federal Government wet-nursing Americans from the time they are born to the time they die. We need Americans who will take care of America so the Government never needs to worry about the people—the welfare of the people.

*   *   *

The Government must begin to withdraw from a whole series of programs that are outside its constitutional mandate—from social-welfare programs, education, public power, agriculture, public housing, urban renewal and all other activities that can be better performed by lower levels of government or by private institutions or by individuals. I do not suggest that the Federal Government drop all of these programs overnight. But I do suggest that we establish by law a rigid timetable for a staged withdrawal.

*   *   *

If we take from a man the personal responsibility for caring for his material needs, we take from him also the will and opportunity to be free.

On Foreign Policy:

We should withdraw diplomatic recognition from all Communist Governments, including that of the Soviet Union.

*   *   *

The Republican Party should announce that victory is our goal in the cold war—not just ending it.

*   *   *

We should make it clear in the most explicit terms that Communist governments are not tolerated in this Hemisphere—and that the Castro regime, being such a Government, will be eliminated. . . . I think we can operate an effective economic blockade of Cuba and I think we can do it at no risk of war.

*   *   *

In nearly every case where we have called upon the United Nations to do our thinking for us . . . we have been a less effective foe of Communism than we otherwise might have been.

*   *   *

Our present policy of not recognizing Red China is eminently right, and the reasons behind that policy apply equally to the Soviet Union and its European satellites.

On Education:

Federal aid to education inevitably means federal control of education.

*   *   *

It is evident . . . that increased school expenditures have more than kept pace with increased school needs.

*   *   *

What could be more ludicrous than the idea that the problem of the quality of education in this country can be solved merely by appropriating very large sums, so we can build bigger and more elaborate facilities?

On Agriculture:

I think we have to arrange some kind of a program that will gradually get the farmer out from under the control of government and subsidies. I don't know how long that would take. I am certain that it would be a terrific economic shock if we dropped it tomorrow. It might take 3 or 4 or 5 years but, at the end of that time, the 30 per cent of agriculture which is now under government would be under the law of supply and demand.

*   *   *

I would start down the hill on agricultural payments. I would stop the 7 billion dollars a year and start getting down to, let's say, 1 billion a year.

*   *   *

I cannot conceive of a more absurd and self-defeating policy than one which subsidizes nonproduction.

*   *   *

The only way to persuade farmers to enter other fields of endeavor is to stop paying inefficient farmers for produce that cannot be sold at free-market prices.

On Social Security and Medicare:

I'll say here that Social Security is a part of our American life. I wish that, when they framed it, they would have made it voluntary. If a man wants it, fine; if he doesn't, he doesn't have to have to take it. But this compulsion—you have to do it—is one of the denials of the freedoms that is very dangerous in this country, because it can be extended.

Any way it is put, the plan . . . for aid to the aged is socialized medicine. What is voluntary about a plan that would entail the participation of every taxpayer whether he wants to or not? What is free about a plan which has the Federal Government intervening in any way at all? Where in the Constitution is the Federal Government given the right to become a federal doctor?

Goldwater's personality and his political views may be of significance to the Republican leaders seeking to win him the nomination. Goldwater himself takes a more sober view. In the late spring of 1963, he told a *Newsweek* reporter: "I ask myself what's my responsibility to conservatism. Is the country really ready for it? If I am beaten at the convention, how much will conservatism be set back?" This does not mean that Senator Goldwater is playing coy about his Presidential ambitions. Very few men within reach of the White House have turned it down. But he realizes that he is the spokesman for a great and vital new movement. Any mistakes he makes will hurt it.

"If I am nominated and roundly beaten by Kennedy, it could be the end of the conservative movement in this country," Goldwater says. "And I'd be through in politics. So if I thought I'd get my tail whipped badly, I'd say the hell with it. But if I ran a reasonably close race—say within a 5 percent plurality—this would be bound to be a brake on the New Frontier philosophy. These things have to be weighed and you can't weighed them accurately now. These factors work on my mind all the time. If there is strength to this grass-roots thing—say, after six months—then there would be time to decide."

If the "grass-roots thing" were a movement financed by special pleaders and inflated by the press, Barry Goldwater would be right. But the "draft Goldwater" movement, though encouraged by the more passionate supporters of the junior senator from Arizona, is in reality a brush fire that can't be stopped. At this point, it is hard to find any devoted conservative Republican who wants to stop it. Thousands of personal letters flood Goldwater's office every week—and if he accepted every plea that he make a personal appearance and speech, he would be at the lectern twenty-four hours a day.

There are no fat-cats behind the Goldwater movement. That the big money goes to a conservative candidate is one of the myths that grew out of the New Deal and has a hard time dying. In any political battle, it is the Liberals who have the biggest plate to pass at the meeting. The "draft Goldwater" partisans have had to beat the bushes energetically to raise enough to set up headquarters, pay for postage and printing, and maintain a salaried staff. There are no foundations and funds from which to draw public relations talent. Volunteers have made up the Goldwater movement, and the professionals will take over only after the nomination is safely in conservative hands.

Meanwhile, the view from the Goldwater camp is not stuffy at all. Barry Goldwater has always had a light touch which shocks the Liberal opposition. If he is working for 18th Century-Fox, as the Liberals sneer, he must have some good scriptwriters with him. "Many predict I might make our finest Civil War President," he said in one speech. "George Romney says he's getting tired of telling people that he's not a candidate for the nomination, and, what's more, he's getting tired of all the traveling he's got to do to tell them." And again: "I will not be a candidate in 1964. There's too much unemployment now and I'd feel very badly if it fell to my lot to put Vaughn Meader out of work."

Barry Goldwater will, I believe, be the candidate. He knows that win or lose, he can break the Liberal Democratic stranglehold on the Congress. He can bring back to the American political system and to the people who vote within its structure a free choice between differing and antagonistic programs. As a conservative, he realizes that the traditional American system of checks and balances must be restored if this country is to remain free. The Willkie-Dewey syndrome almost wrecked the Republican Party and weakened the structure of the Republic. Only a Liberal-conservative confrontation can change that. And history has made Barry

Goldwater the man and the symbol to bring about that confrontation. The cheers which are triggered by the mention of his name at Republican meetings are not accidental. They say that America is once more awake.

XII

KENNEDY *VS.* GOLDWATER

To a United Press International reporter, Barry Goldwater said last summer:

"I don't want this nomination, but it may be forced on me. If I'm put in the position where I have to take it, I won't be a reluctant tiger. I'll get out and fight."

He paused briefly, then added:

"Kennedy is getting weaker and weaker and weaker. People are beginning to react against his inattention to national problems and his indecision. With the right candidate, 1964 could be a Republican year after all."

The key phrase was "with the right candidate." But more significant was the flat statement by a hardheaded practicing politician that "Kennedy is getting weaker and weaker and weaker." Was this simply pre-campaign optimism, or the blindness that afflicts some men as they face the glare of the White House? Kennedy invincibility had seemed assured when Governor Rockefeller was scrambling for the same votes. With Senator Goldwater in seeming control of the nomination, the political prognosis changed drastically. Simply doing the arithmetic, sometimes a deceptive exercise, showed the nature of Kennedy's troubles:

In 1964, the President will need 270 electoral votes.

In 1960, he carried seven of the eleven states of the Confederacy, with 84 electoral votes. If he loses three of these states and does not gain in the North, he will be defeated.

In 1960, Kennedy carried Illinois, Michigan, Minnesota, and Missouri in the Midwest farm belt. In 1964, Michigan has a Republican governor, and the Daley machine in Chicago (which gave him Illinois) is at odds with the Negro and creaking badly. These four states have 69 electoral votes. If he loses Illinois and doesn't pick up any states in the rest of the country, he will be defeated.

In 1960, Kennedy carried eleven states (with 138 electoral votes) by pluralities of less than 51 percent. In 1964, if a half dozen of these close states were to swing over to the Republicans, he would be defeated.

In short, unless there is a great swing to President Kennedy in 1964—and to date the valid indicators have all pointed in the other direction—Kennedy can be swept out of office and still carry New York, New Jersey, and Pennsylvania, and other 1960 strongholds.

If he loses the South, Illinois, and a scattering of the marginal states, Kennedy can be defeated even though he picks up California.

This is the statistical case for Goldwater conservatism. But it presupposes certain facts about the state of Kennedy's popularity and political muscle around the country. In assessing the validity of claims that the President is on the skids, the Gallup Poll is of no value. Even when accurate, it is a plebiscite. The true estimate can come only through an examination of regions and voting groups which form a core of strength in particular regions.

Point One: Can Kennedy hold on to the Negro vote? This would affect his showing in Illinois (Chicago), Michigan (Detroit), and other industrial states. The rise of Negro militancy has created problems which were not foreseen by those who counted on it to keep President Kennedy in office. One of those problems is that Negro leaders want more than the Kennedy Administration can give them. Now they threaten to sit on their hands on election day.

But this is a minor worry. Far more depressing to the Administration is a problem outlined in the New York *Herald Tribune* by Rowland Evans, a very good friend of the Kennedys. In "Inside Report," which he writes with Robert Novak, Evans was brutally realistic:

Other Democratic-inclined minority groups are turning against the Negro. . . . Just what this could mean in lost votes for President Kennedy and other Democrats in 1964 is impossible to say now. But there are enough clues of inter-ethnic hostility to produce sleepless nights for Democratic politicians. . . .

Chicago's young Negro leaders hold [Mayor Richard] Daley responsible for the city's rigidly segregated housing. . . . Irish-Negro hostility is by no means limited to Chicago. In nearly every big city, it threatens the Democratic Party's neat working arrangement under which the Irish provide the leadership and the Negroes supply the votes. Negroes and Irish now find themselves on opposite sides of picket lines as Negroes try to end Jim Crow policies in Irish-dominated construction unions. . . .

Some Irish voters [in Philadelphia], angered by [the Mayor's] concessions to Negroes, may actually switch to the Republican column. . . .

But Irish-Negro hostility is not the only ethnic problem facing Democrats. There is concern among Democratic politicians about growing anti-Semitism in the Negro masses. In Harlem, foɪ instance, it is becoming standard procedure for a Negro leader to prove his militance by dropping some slighting remark about Jews. . . .

Negroes themselves are the target of jealousy by another . . . low status minority—the Spanish-speaking Americans. Such resentment is, in fact, being turned against the Democratic Party in Los Angeles by Mexican-Americans. Although the city's half million Latinos backed Mr. Kennedy overwhelmingly in 1960, their leaders now complain that Democratic leaders have forgotten them in a rush to help Negroes. . . .

This backbiting among minorities discloses some hard truths about the Democrats' ethnic coalition. . . . Far from pulling together for racial equality, minority groups tend to regard each other as competitors.

The Negro trend toward overt anti-Semitism is one that can torpedo Kennedy hopes in November of 1964. If the Jewish community becomes aware of this, its longtime support for Negro civil rights causes will evaporate. The Jewish minority is one which has attained status and economic suppleness. It is well represented in the news media and in the intellectual pursuits. Many of its members are what Madison Avenue calls "opinion makers." Negro anti-Semitic actions will cause them to seek some redress from President Kennedy. And if he refuses, he will gain the chaotic Negro vote but lose the support of Jews who have contributed in works and loyalty to the Democratic cause since the days of Franklin Delano Roosevelt.

Point Two: Is the President in trouble with the farmers? If he is, then he can kiss the election good-bye. The farmers may account for only 8 percent of the population, but they dominate in twenty-two states having a total of 221 electoral votes. (Negroes make up 10 percent of the population but they are concentrated either in already very strong Democratic areas or in the South where their effect on elections as yet is negligible.) Kennedy carried only six of these farming states, and by margins ranging from one percentage point down to three-tenths of a percentage point. And if there is one certainty in the wheat and corn belt, it is that the farmers do not like Secretary of Agriculture Orville Freeman. The wheat referendum demonstrated this, as well as their hatred of controls. Downward fluctuations in wheat prices as the election approaches would be very damaging to Democratic chances. The farmers have not forgotten Kennedy's go-lump-it attitude when the Freeman Control Plan was rejected, or his refusal to propose new legislation to keep prices up. Under Eisenhower, the Democrats made gains in farm-state Senatorial seats and governors' mansions—but by hair-thin pluralities. The Republicans, who now hold more than 50 percent, or 92 out of 175 seats for these states in the House of Representatives, expect to make significant gains.

Point Three: Can he inject enthusiasm into his own party? This is a serious question and perhaps the most important one. With roughly two-thirds of the Congress Democratic, a friendly press, and the sympathy of the intellectual community (whose ideas are far more pervasive than we realize), the New Frontier acts as if it were a besieged army with little hope of rescue. In part, this is due to the early arrogance of the Administration. It was not enough to be a loyal and hard-working Democrat. All the patronage plums, the honors, and the power went to Kennedyites. Close friends and relatives predominated. Those who had been part of the Inner Circle in the Senatorial days—or who had ties with young Robert Kennedy—were the elect of the New Frontier. The others took what they could snatch, but they felt like outsiders. They did not turn against John F. Kennedy—that would have been suicidal. But they were not happy. Even the "in group" had its quick disillusionment. They expected another vital administration, bubbling with inventiveness, full of vigor. And they discovered that some of the New Frontiersmen were still fighting the tired wars of the 1930s while the rest of them were looking for a safe billet. To use Sidney Hyman's phrase, they are now members of "the Party of Silence." And, Hyman said in an article for *Look,* "Why There's Trouble on the New Frontier":

Many of Kennedy's natural friends among the Democrats on Capitol Hill refer to his Administration as "they" not "we." One senator from a Rocky Mountain region, who has braved hostile opinion back home to support the President's program, says of the Administration: "From the way *they* bear themselves, you'd think that the Congressional members of the Democratic Party are a pack of enemy aliens, bent on subverting the way *they* are running things off in a corner."

President Kennedy works hard at winning over the voters and adding dash to the Democratic effort. It has been noted that he delivered more television addresses in his first years in office than Franklin D. Roosevelt made "fireside chats" in an equal period of time. The result, however, has been most discouraging. One letter received by Kennedy after one of his talks reportedly read: "Dear Mr. President: I never knew what Medicare was all about until you spoke last night. Now you've explained it so well, I'm against it."

Point Four: Can Kennedy find adequate explanations for the softening up of the country's foreign policy muscle? Careful pruning of the journalistic bushes has made State Department failures seem like successes. But every day in every way, the facts are becoming known. In the Roosevelt era, it was easy to blame all the failures on the State Department and all the successes on the President. But times have changed—

and the problems are far more pressing than they were in the first two Roosevelt terms. The American people know that it was Kennedy impatience which turned President de Gaulle of France against the United States and Kennedy lack of tact which aggravated the situation to the point that France and America were barely speaking to each other. They have read of the shambles created by the Administration's defense policies in Britain and Canada.

The Cuban situation may not be political fodder by the time the voters go to the polls in 1964. But the methodology of the Kennedy Administration has impinged on the popular consciousness. Cuba remains a sword pointed at the American heart—and the President has done little to blunt its edge or to wrest it from tinhorn dictators like Fidel Castro. The voters remember this though they may be vague on details. The best political analysis would indicate that the Administration's steady harping on the theme "Do you want to risk nuclear war over Cuba?" may have satisfied people—but only for a while. Relief at the continuance of peace is always followed by the question: "How long will this peace last?" The symbol of Neville Chamberlain has yet to be erased from the world's memory.

There are American troops fighting and dying in Vietnam. On the other hand, the Kennedy Administration has refused to realize that there is a linkage with Laos. Kennedy indecision led to the disastrous "troika" there. If Laos goes, then so does Vietnam—and vice versa. The steady decline in the NATO alliance is another case in point. President Kennedy inherited a healthy system. It is now one of the saddest invalids in the diplomatic world. Was this inevitable? Was it happenstance? The voter wants to know, and it may be that in God's good time he will refuse to be put off by an equivocal answer or the rhetoric which silences debate but settles nothing.

Point Five: John F. Kennedy's election was planned on the knowledge that he would be attractive to women. That attraction remains. But surveys made by *Good Housekeeping,* by professional pollster Louis Harris, and by Congressional legislators show that the woman voter has a selective opinion of the Kennedy record. Everywhere the women still oh-and-ah at the Kennedy charm. But they are very frank in their opinion that Kennedy has practiced nepotism to a degree unknown since the days of Rome and favoritism like a latter-day Boss Tweed. Since most American woman handle the family finance, they are also aware that he has done little to reinforce the dollar or to ease the housewife's problem, as the surveys show. They may see the homely virtues of devotion to family in Kennedy, but they do not think he has been a very good President. Choosing in 1960 between the engaging Senator Kennedy and the aloofly introverted Richard Nixon, they found Kennedy the more appealing man. But in a Gold-water-Kennedy confrontation, the choice is different. Even his worst enemies acknowledge the ease and warmth which win people to Barry Goldwater.

Point Six: Can Kennedy point to a record of achievement in domestic affairs? Using a football metaphor, the *New York Times'* James Reston wrote that President Kennedy played "touch government"—he touched a good many problems but tackled very few. (From Reston, these were harsh words.) He has gotten his budgets through in relatively unscathed form —the government has to continue running. But to date his major achievement has been to expand the Federal bureaucracy and to break records in raising the national debt. The promises of getting the country "on the move" and of stimulating economic growth have not materialized—and the "innovations" which were to be introduced to bring this about have turned out to be slightly refurbished 1933 New Deal slogans and a great amount of palaver. Except for the new faces in government offices, the mixture is as before. For two sessions, Congressional Democrats have looked for leadership and inspiration. But the Kennedy operation on the Hill—as the Democrats themselves privately aver—has been one of deals and pressure. There has been not a single burst of enthusiasm over domestic policy since January 1961.

Regarding defense, Kennedy has convinced large segments of Congress and an increasing number of voters that he is determined to preside over the liquidation of the United States armed forces. A group of slide-rule-wielding "whiz kids" have taken over the Pentagon. They have unceremoniously pushed aside the military and taken on such functions as the evaluation of weapons systems—something they were not taught at the Ivy League colleges from which they sprang. Morale in the services is low—and for a reason. Since the Kennedy take-over, the United States has not produced a single new weapons system. It has, however, begun the dismantling of the Strategic Air Command. The missile program, which provides the nation with its major defense system, was all on paper and in the works before Kennedy took office. Having urged that we put all our NATO eggs in the Polaris basket—and having begun to shut down U. S. missile bases abroad—the Administration now has begun to drag its feet in the production of nuclear submarines, deciding on less than the Congress was more than willing to pay for.

The space program, also in the works when President Eisenhower drove away from the White House in January of 1961, has fared fantastically well. But for reasons unknown, Kennedy has continued to play it down and to reiterate what is patently not so—that the United States is "second best" in space. (The only accurate statement would be that we are different in space, but that scientifically and from the standpoint of control we are far ahead. As of this writing, no American astronaut has burned up in space, whereas our Intelligence grudgingly admits that at least a dozen Russians have lost their lives in the cold blue yonder.)

Point Seven: There is often a great gap between what is so and what people believe to be so. And in this psychological gray area between the shadow and the substance, the Kennedy Administration has also been hurt among its once most-ardent endorsers. Again, Sidney Hyman:

> "Justice" has lost its motive power as the source and object of politics [under Kennedy]. Few people in Washington today even mention the word. Justice, after all, has an up-and-at-'em ring. It implies that something ought to be done about social problems close at hand . . . problems about which the Census Bureau has masses of precise data. Yet a number of New Frontiersmen seem to believe that one should not press too hard. Why? Because the pressure could split the country, and, as everyone knows, monolithic unity alone will win the cold war against the monolithic Communists. So don't talk about justice. . . . The great thing to do, instead, is to talk about "power" and "efficiency." These are the great unifying words of the hour, used to explain any action —or inaction—in dealing with Castro and Khrushchev, Laos and South Vietnam, de Gaulle and Adenauer.

Here is a Liberal describing the New Frontier—and he is not alone. Prince Hamlet in the White House has not pleased those who accepted Bobby Kennedy's rather ominous words to a caucus at the 1960 convention: "We're a young group that's going to take over the country." There are great flurries of activity from time to time, but carrying the Hamlet analogy forward, it should be recalled that the melancholy Dane in one such burst killed his friend Polonius.

The Gallup Polls reflect this lack of identification with the Kennedy Administration, the "they" feeling described by Hyman. Kennedy would like to walk in Franklin Roosevelt's shoes, but he has earned neither the love nor the hatred inspired by him. In the Roosevelt era, it was a "we" feeling all along. In the confrontation to come, this may be the single most important factor. Many Americans can forget ideological issues when caught up in the quadrennial excitement, voting for the man. In Barry Goldwater, the till-now alienated conservatives will have a candidate they can support wholeheartedly. The uncommitted will have a candidate who imparts that "we" feeling, who can set a crowd to cheering as no Republican has done since the days of Teddy Roosevelt. Young people who have reached voting age in the last two or three years do not care about tired, thirty-year-old feuds. They are more than slightly chagrined at the efforts of some New Frontiersmen to make America a kind of second-class Ferdinand the Bull. They are bored with a mechanistic, materialistic view of history and society. They can therefore rise to the challenge thrown down by Barry Goldwater when he addressed the Young Republicans in June of 1963:

It is time we realized more clearly that the modern "liberals" who are hopelessly confined to an economic view of man, who are hopeless captives of the big-city machines of the North, are not only morally bankrupt but they are also intellectually bankrupt.

They have not had a new idea in thirty years . . .

They are sterile and rigid.

Modern "liberalism" is only a form of rigor mortis.

In 1964, and in elections to come, the choice will be between conservatism and Liberalism, between a soaring view of the American future and a niggling concept of our destiny, between the free prosperity that men make for themselves and the shackled security that their governments may dole out to them. The choice will be between the speakers of truth and the muddiers of public policy who intone that conservatism is nothing but extremism—and extremism subversion more dangerous than the vast Communist conspiracy.

The New Frontier is Lilliput. Conservatism is the City of Freedom.

The choice is clear.